LifeBuilders Leadership Certification

Manual

ISBN: 978-1-940682-26-6

Special Thanks

Special thanks to giants of the faith and pioneers of Men's Ministry, who laid a solid foundation to reach and disciple men. Patrick Morley said,

> "To get **society** right . . .
> Get the **Church** right; to get the church right,
> Get **Families** right; to get families right,
> Get **marriages** right; to get marriages right,
> Get **Men** right."

Special thanks and appreciation to:

The Church of God Executive Committee for recognizing the importance of reaching and discipling men and providing leadership through structural transition that made Men's Discipleship a priority.

Current & Previous Committee: Mark Williams, David Griffis, J. David Stephens, Wallace Sibley, Thomas Propes, Raymond Culpepper, Tim Hill

Dr. John D. Nichols who was instrumental in the establishment of Men's Ministry, first known in the Church of God as Men's Fellowship.

Charles Beach for outstanding leadership in founding the first Men's Fellowship in the Church of God.

Leonard Albert, who served the Church of God as Director of Men's Ministries from 1975-2010.

Don Warrington for outstanding contributions in writing and developing resources for discipling men.

Ed Cole a key leader whose vision and compassion for men continues to rescue and disciple men.

Key Ministry Partners

Patrick Morley, Founder and CEO of Man in the Mirror.

Paul Cole, President of Christian Men's Network Worldwide.

Darrel Billups, President of the National Coalition of Men's Ministries.

Table of Contents

SECTION 1

Introduction

Welcome to LifeBuilders, Men Empowered By The Spirit . . .

You are embarking on a journey of transformation, discipleship, spiritual warfare, and mission. Making disciples requires great faith, spiritual strength, and perseverance but that is the mission given to us by God, Who is able to do exceeding, abundantly, above all that we ask or think! You will face great challenges but the rewards are greater. Men's lives will be changed. Sons and daughters will have a dad who loves God and disciples them in God's grace. Wives will have godly husbands who love them as Christ loved the Church. Families, churches, communities and our world will be changed as a result of your ministry.

My dad was an alcoholic. I know the pain of growing up with a dad who was a slave to alcohol. Please don't misunderstand. I loved my dad. He was a kind, loving man who was known for helping the less fortunate. I remember the tears as he begged for my forgiveness and promised to never drink again. Men like my dad need help. Churches are filled with men who have never experienced the transforming grace of God that sets them free from the bondage of sin. Too many men have never discovered the joys of following Christ fully and embracing their God given destiny. Someone asked, why doesn't God do something. God did something! He gave His only begotten Son to die in our place. He sent the Holy Spirit to convict, transform, sanctify and empower men to become disciples who make disciples. God did something! He called you and is sending you and me to disciple men.

You are embarking on a mission to rescue men, to help men discover the healing grace of God, to help men become the men of God they were created to be and to raise up an army of men with a mission, equipped to disciple other men. It is true that many churches have failed to reach men or produce men disciples. The moral dilemmas of our culture are witness to the fact that churches have failed to disciple men. This mission is bigger than you are. This is the mission of God. However, you have a promise, "And it shall come to pass in the last days, says God, that I will pour out of My Spirit on all flesh; your sons and your daughters shall prophesy, your young men shall see visions, your old men shall dream dreams" (Acts 2:17). Expect the anointing of the Holy Spirit to empower you to help men discover God's grace and be set free from the bondages of sin to become the men of God they were born to be.

This training is to prepare you for the mission. Failure is not an option!

Go forward in great faith, knowing that we have reason to have confidence in God who gives us the victory through our Lord, Jesus Christ. I am praying for you.

—David H. Gosnell
International Men's Discipleship Coordinator

Why Your Church Needs a LifeBuilders Men's Discipleship Ministry

Strong churches are made up of strong men! A LifeBuilders Men's Discipleship Ministry will make disciples, benefit the men, and the local church and its pastor.

Benefits for the Men

- Disciples men through mentoring, small groups, spiritual disciplines and mission.

- Equips and trains men for ministry by helping them discover and use their spiritual gifts.

- Mobilizes men for work in the church by emphasizing that "everyone is a minister" and, therefore, a witness for Jesus Christ.

- Enables men to experience spiritual renewal through personal Bible study, group Bible studies, interaction, development of an effective prayer life, and empowerment for witnessing and serving through the baptism in the Holy Spirit.

- Provides men encouragement, accountability, and a sense of belonging through organized Christian fellowship with other men in the church and helps maintain their commitment to the church family.

- Encourages men to be better husbands, fathers, providers, and spiritual leaders as priests in the home and Christian workers and businessmen in the workplace.

- Provides a central purpose of mission.

- Organizes prayer support for the pastor and vital ministries of the church.

Benefits for the Pastor

- Provides support for the pastor.

- Provides able and wise leadership to help the pastor.

- Develops men to do the work of ministry.

- Provides prayer support through the Pastor's Prayer Partners program.

LifeBuilders Certification Program

The LifeBuilders Leadership Certification Program is designed to train LifeBuilders leaders and teams.

You will learn:

Why your church needs a LifeBuilders discipleship ministry.

Keys to starting a LifeBuilders discipleship ministry.

The need and qualities of a strong LifeBuilders ministry leader.

How to build and train your LifeBuilders ministry team.

How to get off to a good start.

How to build ministry momentum.

How to build entry points for men into your LifeBuilders discipleship ministry.

Keys to maintaining a quality LifeBuilders discipleship ministry.

How to disciple men.

How to be connected for ministry effectiveness.

How to build and implement a Pastor's Prayer Partner ministry.

How to train Transformational Discipleship small group leaders.

And discover ministry resources and discipleship initiatives to disciple men.

Certification Program Requirements

This section is provided for the purpose of defining the requirements to receive and maintain LifeBuilders Leadership Certification.

Level 1 LifeBuilders Leadership Certification may be attained by meeting the following criteria:

1. Read the LifeBuilders Leadership Certification Manual.

2. Complete the review at the end of the Certification Manual. (It is recommended that the local church certification process be completed in a small group setting.)

3. Have a Pastor's Confidential Endorsement signed by your senior pastor including verification of a criminal background check.

4. Have up-to-date LifeBuilders Charter and Leadership Team Forms at the International Men's Discipleship office. Participation in a chartered LifeBuilders discipleship ministry is required to obtain certification.

Level 2 LifeBuilders Leaders Certification may be attained by meeting the following criteria:

1. Complete the requirements for Level 1 Certification.

2. Attend a LifeBuilders Leadership Certification Conference.

Men who have attended a LifeBuilders Leadership Certification Conference will be certified at Level 2 and are certified to teach and certify local leaders. Certification forms will be provided by the International LifeBuilders Men's Discipleship office.

Level 3 LifeBuilders Leaders Certification

This is reserved for State/Regional LifeBuilders/Men's Discipleship Leaders and State/Region LifeBuilders Team Members. Leaders with Level 3 Certification may conduct LifeBuilders Leadership Training Conferences and certify both Level 1 and Level 2 leaders. Level 3 Certification assumes a partnership with International LifeBuilders Discipleship Ministries and participation in the LifeBuilders Leadership Network. Level 3 Certification and LifeBuilders Leadership Network is designed to be a coaching network to assist with the development and implementation of State/Regional LifeBuilders Initiative to disciple men. Appointment by state/regional bishop is validation of qualifications for Level 3 leaders. Verification of state/regional team members will be processed with the forms and endorsement of the state/regional LifeBuilders leader.

Forms may be returned to:

Church of God International Offices
Men's Discipleship
P.O. Box 2430
Cleveland, TN 37320

Or by email at:

Mensdiscipleship@churchofgod.org

SECTION 2

Keys to Starting A LifeBuilders Discipleship Ministry
Quick Start Guide

1. **Support from the pastor.** Whatever LifeBuilders men's ministries is able to do in accomplishing its task will, to a great degree, depend on the attitude, leadership, support, relationship, and assistance given by the pastor. The pastor is vital to men's ministry work. He stands with the team in giving direction and promotion. The pastor can influence the men to help accomplish the total mission of the church. Every word of support from the pastor publically is of vast importance to the success of the ministry.

2. **Establish a clear mission and vision.** Jesus said, "All authority has been given to Me in heaven and on earth. Go therefore and make disciples of all the nations, baptizing them in the name of the Father and of the Son and of the Holy Spirit, teaching them to observe all things that I have commanded you; and lo, I am with you always, even to the end of the age" (Matthew 28:18-20). The vision is for every nation, which includes every man to be a disciple. Jesus said, "A disciple is not above his teacher, but everyone who is perfectly trained will be like his teacher" (Luke 6:40). It is God's will that every person be saved and be a faithful follower of Christ becoming more like him daily.

    Men who are faithful followers of Jesus Christ will be better husbands, fathers, leaders, followers, members, etc. Our mission is making disciples.

3. **Have a strong LifeBuilders leader.** LifeBuilders ministry is not a one-person operation but make no mistake, the LifeBuilders leader is vital to the success or failure of the ministry. LifeBuilders ministry will never rise above the leader. Strong passionate leadership for discipling men is vital for a successful ministry.

4. **Build a LifeBuilders leadership team.** God is moving in the hearts of men. He is calling men to stand up for what they believe in—to be faithful in their personal walk with Christ, to their families and to their church. In order to begin an effective ministry to men in your church or to revive your existing men's ministry, you need to assemble a team of dedicated people to organize and lead the effort. Sometimes it is possible to attract men to the local church through exciting events or conferences. We call these "momentum creating events." Years of experience tells us that the only way to keep these men involved is to provide a well-planned, ongoing local church men's ministry with clear purposes and credible people involved.

5.   **Train the LifeBuilders leadership team.** Train the team, using the *LifeBuilders Leadership Certification Manual*. LifeBuilders certified leaders will be provided certificates to present to leaders who complete the training in the local church. Team members who complete the training will receive a Level 1 Certification.

6.   **Lead your leadership team through a small group study**: *LifeBuilders Essentials*, or *James: A Path to Discipleship*, and this *LifeBuilders Leadership Certification Manual*.

     Leading the team through a small group study using the Transformational Discipleship Group Model will strengthen relationships, develop missional leaders and model effective small group ministry that will be duplicated many times over.

     Leading the LifeBuilders Leadership Team in the discipleship process is vital to the long-term success of the ministry.

7.   **Schedule a leadership team kickoff meeting.** Now that you have your men's leaders recruited, trained, and in place its time to release them to lead. The ways in which these men are released become a model for the way they release others who will work under them. Always remember that the senior pastor or his appointee is always invited to be a part of this and any other gathering.

8.   **Charter your local LifeBuilders discipleship ministry** with Church of God International LifeBuilders' office. You can charter by using the Charter Form in the back of this manual or online at coglifebuilders.com/lifebuilders_forms.htm.

9.   **Select and train small group teachers** and prepare to launch groups using the Transformational Discipleship Group Strategy.

10. **Launch Transformational Small Groups** (Section 8)

11. **Plan big events to create momentum** for LifeBuilders ministry

12. **Start monthly LifeBuilders meetings.** The regular meeting is important as part of building a "sustainable" men's ministry. By having regular meetings, the momentum of the chapter is energized. It's also important for fellowship purposes and getting feedback for ministry improvement. By "regular" meetings we mean a monthly meeting. Failure to meet consistently makes the momentum difficult to sustain.

13. **Launch Pastor's Prayer Partners.** The monthly meeting is a good place to launch the Pastor's Prayer Partner Program. This program is included in resource section of this manual.

Summary

The Chinese have many beautiful sayings. One goes like this: *Do not fear going forward slowly. Fear only to stand still.* We do not have the luxury of waiting. We are now in a life-and-death battle for the souls of men. We live in a fallen world, but God is more powerful than that fallen world. With an effective LifeBuilders Men's Discipleship leadership team we can help men break free from Satan's grip through the power of Christ and lead them to discover God's destiny for their lives and families. We can help keep men safe from the pain and grief that sin brings. We can help men do excellent ministry in the church.

We believe that it is a winnable battle if we move forward now to reach, train, and equip men for ministry. This is an exciting and fruit-producing mission! Oh yes, here is another ancient Chinese proverb: *The best time to plant a tree was 20 years ago . . . the next best time is now.*

Let's get started!

SECTION 3

The LifeBuilders Initiative

Questions and Important Issues

If most of us really stop and think about the history of men's ministry, it will boil down to one thing—events. The events approach, however, has two major problems.

One is that we cannot live in events 24/7. Sooner or later we have to come off the "mountain top" and dwell with our lives—our families, our jobs, our communities, our church. Even an event like receiving the law on top of Mount Sinai had fading glory: "Moses . . . covered his face with a veil, to prevent the Israelites from gazing at the disappearance of what was passing away" (2 Corinthians 3:13).

The second problem is that the New Testament doesn't support the idea of an event-driven ministry or even an event-driven church. There were great events: the Day of Pentecost, Paul's encounter with Jesus on the road to Damascus, and more. But the growth of the church took place between these events also: "And the Lord daily added to their company those who were in the path of salvation" (Acts 2:47).

Does Your Church Welcome Men?

On the surface, that may sound like a really stupid question. But let's think about it. What kind of message does your church send to a man the first time, and every time thereafter, (if it has more chances) he comes into your church?

Let's start with the basics—the appearance and décor of your church. Is it frilly and feminine? What kinds of colors are being used? One ministry leader walked into the rest room of one church organization, only to turn and flee. Why? The men's room was so feminine in appearance that he instantly panicked because he thought he was in the wrong rest room! Most churches are decorated solely by their women, which is great except that they usually don't take into consideration that men's and women's tastes are simply different.

Then we turn to the congregation. Does your congregation dress formally? This varies widely by culture—and your church needs to be mindful of the culture(s) it's ministering to. The current trend in the U.S.A. is towards less formal dress. Workplaces have relaxed their dress codes, but many churches have not.

Then there's the music. Seattle Pastor Mark Driscoll stated that he preferred the traditional hymns to the more contemporary "CCLI" material because the latter was, in his estimation, for soccer moms in minivans! Much of Christian music today represents a love song to God. Although Christianity is a religion driven by God's love for us, and we cannot get to heaven unless we love God, women more freely express their praise to God as a love song than men do, for obvious reasons.

Also consider the preaching. Most ministers have been trained in a "three points and a conclusion" organization for their sermons. But men prefer to concentrate on one thing at a time, so while the minister is off on points 2 and 3 (and whatever other digressions he or she gets into) the men are still trying to absorb point 1, if they are still interested.

Finally, if a man gets through all this and a man sticks with the church, does the church really value him? Or does it just want what it can get out of him, in terms of time, talent, and money? Men want to achieve, not just fulfill tasks. "Theirs not to reason why, theirs but to do and die" may have been good enough for the Light Brigade (they in fact, lost about a fourth of their number) but it won't work for men today.

Evangelical churches pride themselves in becoming "all things to all men, so as at all costs to save some" (1 Corinthians 9:22). The content of the message that is communicated to men is referred to as the church's "man code," and every church has one, consciously or not. What's yours?

Discipleship: The Portal Priority

Pentecostal theology in general and the Church of God in particular tells us that there's more to the Christian life than fire insurance. We used to speak regularly of people getting "saved, sanctified, baptized in the Holy Ghost and joining the Church of God." Each of those events needs to be seen as a milestone in one's Christian walk.

But to get from one milestone to another—and ultimately the destination—there needs to be a road. That road is discipleship, and making it the core of your program for men is the key to making that program sustainable. Jesus Christ set the pattern for all of us with His life and ministry. That can be broken down into three phases:

1. Jesus–God himself–came to earth and invested three years in those whom He chose.

2. Jesus Christ rose from the dead, and gave the first and foremost order to his soon to be apostles: "Therefore go and make disciples of all the nations, baptizing them into the Faith of the Father, the Son, and the Holy Spirit, And teaching them to lay to heart all the commands that I have given you; and, remember, I myself am with you every day until the close of the age" (Matthew 28:19-20). Making disciples, therefore, is our core mission.

3. On the Day of Pentecost, the apostles received the baptism (and the empowerment) of the Holy Spirit to carry out that mission. They finally understood the nature of Jesus' mission to this earth, which is reflected in Peter's confident and informed preaching. But a process of discipleship preceded that event of power.

There's no reason to think that the plan has changed: Jesus' final command was to make disciples, and it makes sense that we need to make it our "portal priority." A portal priority is the doorway to our other tasks, and discipleship is clearly that.

It's especially important in men's ministries. Men instinctively dislike being micromanaged. It's essential, therefore, to internalize God's presence and understanding: "Thy word have I hid in mine heart, that I might not sin against thee" (Psalm 119:11). That process is discipleship.

Wide to Deep

The whole idea of progress in the Christian life implies that different people are at different points. That's true for the men in your church. Each one of them is at a different point in his walk with God. If you include all the men in your church (and you should) and those to whom your church reaches out, then each one of them is at a different point in his walk with God. But isn't the whole point to get them into a deeper, or closer walk with God? It sure is! But before that you need to minister to the men where they are, and from there draw them into a more "in depth" relationship. That process is referred to as "wide to deep" and organizing your men's ministry around it is crucial to your success.

We said at the start that events don't make a men's ministry. But events can and should be used to further the process of discipleship, even when that process precedes a man actually coming to Christ. Each event, however, has its primary appeal to a man at a different point in his walk with God. A golf tournament, for example, will appeal to a man just becoming interested in the church, whereas a 16-week Bible study requires a higher level of commitment. (The golf tournament, however, is probably a tougher test of one's sanctification!)

In this book we will present many event suggestions. At those events which are "wide"; i.e., geared towards those new to the church or Christianity, it's important to extend an invitation to events which are "deep," or more accurately deeper. In this way the events are used to draw men into a closer walk with God. Thus the events become a tool of ministry rather than the ministry being merely a series of events.

Once the chapter is organized, a good way to start things off is to find out where you are. As men's ministry leaders, it's tempting to get up and proclaim, "Thus sayeth the Lord . . ." and put the program for the men's ministry in front of them. But you as men's leaders may soon find out that the program that you were sure came "from the heart of God" didn't come with the men to carry it out!

One way to avoid this result—or give you some idea of what kind of training your men need to bring them into a full service—is to survey the men for their spiritual gifts. Doing this brings us to an important issue you must come to terms with as a leader of men: why are men in Christ different from each other? Or me?

You've probably asked yourself, "If we all have received the same Jesus Christ as Savior and have the same Holy Spirit working in our lives, why are we as Christians so different when it comes to spiritual matters? Why are we not all motivated by the same sermon, cause, or react the same way to situations?" As hard as it is to understand at times, God has given us different ministry gifts and it is this difference working in harmony that gives us our uniqueness. Salvation does not clone us! Notice we said *difference but working in harmony*. Our body parts have different functions but all work together for the good of the body.

Leading people into Christian discipleship is the major task of church leaders. An important part of discipleship growth has to do with preparation and involvement in ministry. This is where spiritual gifts come in because they are the unique endowments of the Spirit that makes effective ministry possible.

Building an Effective LifeBuilders Ministry

The Pastor's Role

Whatever LifeBuilders Men's Ministries is able to do in accomplishing its task will, to a great degree, depend on the attitude, support, relationship, and assistance given by the pastor. The pastor is vital to men's ministry work. He stands with the team in giving direction and promotion. The pastor can influence the men to help accomplish the total mission of the church.

Important responsibilities of the pastor are to:

- Initiate the selection of team leaders and discipleship team. The pastor can use whatever resources are at his or her disposal to choose capable men.

- Oversee discipleship process of the LifeBuilders leader and leadership team. One of the greatest responsibilities and privileges of a pastor is to disciple and train the leadership team. Jesus modeled this approach. Jesus called the disciples to follow Him. He called them to Himself and ordained them, that they might be with Him" (Mark 3:13-19). These are men who will disciple and develop leaders for the future.

- Provide guidance. The pastor should actively assist the ministry team in planning the goals and work of the group.

- Encourage participation. The pastor should involve men in the total ministry of the church.

- Organize a Prayer Partners Team. This gives men an opportunity to participate in prayer with the pastor.

- Sponsor activities for men. Encourage the men to take advantage of district, state and national men's ministry events and conferences.

> The senior pastor or a personal delegate is
> always an "ex-officio" member
> at all LifeBuilders Men's Discipleship meetings.

Establish a clear mission and vision.

Jesus said, "All authority has been given to Me in heaven and on earth. Go therefore and make disciples of all the nations, baptizing them in the name of the Father and of the Son and of the Holy Spirit, teaching them to observe all things that I have commanded you; and lo, I am with you always, even to the end of the age" (Matthew 28:18-20). The vision is every nation, which includes every person a disciple. Jesus said, "A disciple is not above his teacher, but everyone who is perfectly trained will be like his teacher" (Luke 6:40). It is God's will that every person be saved and a faithful follower of Christ becoming more like Him daily.

Men who are faithful followers of Jesus Christ will be better husbands, fathers, leaders, followers, members, etc. Our mission is making disciples.

Discipleship of men does not just happen. The typical Evangelical church has a women-men ratio of 3-2, or worse 2-1. Many pastors and laity accept this as a way of life without giving it much thought, let alone effort to remedy the problem. They simply allow whatever men's group the church has—assuming it has one at all—go on as "ROMEOS:" Real Old Men Eating Out on Saturday.

Yet studies show that a saved man is crucial in winning his entire household to the Lord. If a woman becomes a Christian, 17 percent of the time she will lead her family to Christ. If her child passes from death to life first, 31 percent of the time he or she will lead the family to Christ. But, if the man of the house becomes a Christian, 94 percent of the time the rest of the household will follow his lead to eternal life. Beyond that, studies have also shown that men are crucial in transmitting the Christian faith to the next generation.

Strong Leadership is Vital

LifeBuilders Men's Discipleship is not a one-person operation, but make no mistake, the LifeBuilders leader is vital to the success or failure of the ministry. Your LifeBuilders ministry will never rise above the leader.

Nine Vital Characteristics of a LifeBuilders Leader

1. **He must have a testimony.** The LifeBuilders leader must be born again, transformed by the grace of God, saved and be passionate about his relationship with Jesus Christ. He must be willing to share his story of God's transforming grace in his life. No one is perfect and that is not the issue.

   I recommend that every leader write his testimony and be able to share it in one minute or less. God will use your testimony to touch many lives. Men feel isolated and have a sense of hopelessness. The story of God's grace brings hope and God uses it to bring transformation to men. Tell your story. Make your story as simple as ABC:

   a. What was your life like before you came to Christ?

   b. How did you come to Christ?

   c. What difference has coming to Christ meant in your life and for your family?

   Teach your leadership team to know their story and share it often. Hearing your story will open the door for new men to be comfortable and allow them to see hope for their lives through Jesus Christ.

2. **He must be a disciple.** You cannot take men where *you* are unwilling to go. Discipleship is more than participating in events or learning a curriculum. Discipleship is a life of walking with Christ and drawing close to Him. Discipleship means that you are changing and growing in Christ.

3. **He must be a man of the Word.** Research indicates that one of the most important factors in spiritual growth, regardless of what place you are, is the Word of God. I am not talking about hearing a sermon. Yes, sermons and preaching are important. I am talking about your personal time with the Lord reading and studying His Word.

   It is important to begin with a clear understanding that the Bible is God's Word. I enjoy reading books about the Bible but our greatest need is not to read what people say about the Bible but to read the Bible and hear God speak directly to us through His Word and the Holy Spirit. When we study God's Word, we should expect to encounter Him. I encourage you to learn to study the Bible for yourself using the Inductive Method. The Bible is God's Word. The Holy Spirit will lead you, and bring change in your life through the study of His Word.

   Read the Word of God. Study the Word of God. Your faith will grow. Your passion for Christ will grow. Your sensitivity to the Holy Spirit will grow. Your love for others will grow. Read Psalm 119 and you will discover how powerful God's Word is. Three questions are important: What does the Bible say? What does it mean? What am I supposed to do?

The apostle Paul said, "All Scripture is given by inspiration of God, and is profitable for doctrine, for reproof, for correction, for instruction in righteousness, that the man of God may be complete, thoroughly equipped for every good work" (2 Timothy 3:16-17).

The writer of Hebrews said, "For the word of God is living and powerful, and sharper than any two-edged sword, piercing even to the division of soul and spirit, and of joints and marrow, and is a discerner of the thoughts and intents of the heart" (Hebrews 4:12).

"Faith comes by hearing and hearing by the Word of God" (Romans 10:17).

"Study to shew thyself approved unto God, a workman that needeth not to be ashamed, rightly dividing the word of truth" (2 Timothy 2:15 KJV).

4. **He must be a man of prayer.** One of the most overlooked keys in the discipleship process is prayer. Jesus called the disciples to Himself and ordained them that they might be with Him. Then, He sent them out to preach and heal the sick and to minister. LifeBuilders leaders are on the front line of ministry. You cannot help people be delivered from the clutches of the devil through your own ingenuity. You must be a man of prayer. Your leadership team will be blessed with different ministry gifts and talents but each of them must be a man of prayer.

5. **He must be led by the Holy Spirit.** It is impossible to teach and disciple men without the power of the Holy Spirit. He, the Holy Spirit, will lead you and guide you and empower you to touch the lives of men. Learn to be sensitive to the Holy Spirit in every aspect of your ministry to men.

6. **He must be a worshipper.** When men respond to an altar call, be the first one there to pray with them.

7. **He must be faithful to God** in the church and a testimony outside of the church.

8. **He must be passionate about reaching and discipling men.**

9. **He must allow God to develop his leadership gifts.**

Build a Strong LifeBuilders Team

God is moving in the hearts of men. He is calling men to stand up for what they believe in—to be faithful in their personal walk with Christ, to their families and to their church. In order to begin an effective ministry to men in your church or to revive your existing men's ministry, you need to assemble a team of dedicated people to organize and lead the effort. Sometimes it is possible to attract men to the local church through exciting events or conferences. We call these "momentum-creating events." Years of experience tells us that the only way to keep these men involved is to provide a well-planned, on-going local church men's discipleship ministry with clear purposes and credible people involved. This section shows how to find the men who will lead other men in the local church.

Campus Crusade for Christ founder, Bill Bright, often said, "Everything boils down to leadership." Dr. Pat Morley, founder of Man in the Mirror Ministries says, "The height of your men's ministry will be determined by the depth of your leadership."

The truth is that in order to begin and/or sustain an effective ministry to men and disciple new ones, you will need to put together a small group of dedicated leaders who truly want to see the church minister to men. Someone has to organize and lead the effort. It is essential to choose your leaders wisely. You will need to choose not only a team leader, but a whole team if you want to reach and disciple men. Reaching men through other men using groups and teams is God's idea. In the Old Testament, King David had his mighty men, Jesus recruited and trained 12 disciples, and the early church had deacons, elders and lay ministers. The same is true today—you need an organized force to reach men—a band of brothers with an arrow through their heart for men's ministry in the local church. Let's look at a strategy to find them.

Identify the Men Who Can Lead

There are basically three types of leaders: (1) those who are now involved, (2) those who are in training to become leaders, and (3) those who feel that God is calling them in this area. This brings us to a present truth: your leaders don't have to start out committed—that can come later. Here are the steps involved:

1. Prayerfully write out a list of the ten or twelve most spiritually respected men in your church.

    a. At this point it doesn't matter how busy their schedule is or even if they are interested or not.

    b. Focus on men who have a heart for God and for reaching others. Let them make up their own minds under God's leadership.

    c. The idea is to identify and equip a men's discipleship ministry leadership team who will in turn produce cutting-edge ministry opportunities for the men. Pray for God to give you favor with these perspective candidates.

2. Look for individual leadership team members who have one or more of these abilities:

a. **Salespeople.** These men are the "persuaders" because they know how to get other people excited about an idea. They are forever salespeople because it is just in them to try to persuade others to join in on a plan or idea. They are great to have on your team because, by instinct, they help others feel the excitement of the challenge and they convey the spirit of "we can do this" when it comes to ministry.

b. **Doers.** These are the men who can "cut to the chase" and get the job done. They are front-line guys who, as we say, can "deliver the mail." They have the skills to deliver ministry so tasks are completed properly and on time.

c. **Administrators.** These are the men that possess the natural talent to coordinate, plan and troubleshoot. They have the ability to see "what's coming down the pike" and be proactive in helping solve potential problems. They not only do the work, but because they are leaders, they uphold others who also are working.

Meet personally with each potential leader to get better acquainted, share your heart to disciple men and invite him to pray with you about LifeBuilders ministry. During your personal meeting with potential leaders, you might approach each of them and say something like this: "God has put it on my mind to explore the need and desirability of starting (or reorganizing) a LifeBuilders men's discipleship ministry in our church. I believe you are one of a handful of men that the other men in our church would follow. I want to have a meeting to discuss the possibilities. Would you be willing to pray about coming to this one meeting and give your counsel?" It is quite possible that not all will respond positively, but hopefully, five or six of the men will step forward for possible leadership positions.

Schedule a Preliminary Meeting

Pointers for the first meeting:

1. Keep the first meeting to a maximum of one hour. If everyone knows it's a one-hour meeting, you can be very productive. Besides, a long, tiring meeting may create second thoughts about going further.

2. In preparation for this initial meeting, you will want to share your vision for the men of the church. It is important to understand that the ultimate purpose of any LifeBuilders men's discipleship ministry is to reach and win men to Christ and to disciple them into an authentic Christ-centered relationship. As you put together a vision statement for your men's ministry, you want to be specific enough so that others capture a sense of where the ministry is going. Yet you want to be loose enough with details, so that you can easily incorporate creative new ideas as new leaders join the team.

3. Try to answer these questions before the meeting:

a. What is the main goal we'll accomplish through this ministry?

b. Why do we want a men's ministry in the church? (Hint: see #2 above.)

c. What methods will we use—what is our philosophy of ministry?

d. How will we create, capture, and sustain momentum among our men?

e. Do we have ideas about what activities and programs we might incorporate into our ministry?

f. How can we demonstrate that a healthy men's ministry will strengthen the whole church?

4. Meeting content:

a. Begin with prayer (about five minutes).

b. Review the history of ministry to men in your church (about five minutes).

c. Be up front and honest about the blessing and the burdens of previous attempts at men's ministry.

d. Share the potential of a new or renewed LifeBuilders men's discipleship. Our new LifeBuilders plan with an emphasis on discipleship will renew your men's ministry because many men will be won to Christ, discipled and by extension, bless the families in our church and community.

e. Talk a little about the present environment for reaching men (about 15 minutes).

- How are men doing?
- What are their problems?
- How should the church respond?

f. Review our LifeBuilders discipleship materials (about 15 minutes). Talk about the potential of discipling and training the men of your church.

g. Closing comments:

"It seems clear that God is calling us to reach the men of our church and help them grow. I would like to suggest that, together, we go through a three-week process of designing a men's ministry for our church using the Church of God LifeBuilders men's discipleship material as a guide. Who would like to give it a try?"

Responsibilities for Leadership Team Members

Later on in this manual we explain in detail some of the specific duties of the men's discipleship team members. At this point it is important to consider the "big picture" of your ministry to men and look at some general areas that will need leadership from the team. Keep in mind that these individual men can recruit other men to work with them thus forming a small group or team. Here's a list:

1. **Strategy and Coordination.** This man is responsible for focusing on strategic (overall, long-term) issues of the ministry. He helps define identity, themes, and priorities at the ministry level. He offers advice about the overall direction of the LifeBuilders ministry to men. This person works with the LifeBuilders team leader to plan the conferences, seminars, and ministry events for the men of the church.

2. **Community.** This member helps develop a sense of "male friendliness" in the church. He finds ways to make male visitors feel at home when they visit the church services. This person will provide various entry points where both newcomers and seasoned attendees feel comfortable, connected, inspired, and transformed. He actively welcomes and greets individuals at men's functions. He also provides follow-up and coordination for people interested in getting involved in other areas of ministry. This man is responsible for the publishing of a men's monthly email or printed newsletter.

3. **Prayer and Intercession.** This man leads the prayer effort with intercession for people, plans, and activities for the men. He provides a prayer covering and is available to pray with other teams or men's groups. He will be the point man for the "Pastor's Prayer Partner" program (explained later on in this manual).

4. **Team Leader.** LifeBuilders men's discipleship has developed a plan to train a key leader in each local church to help coach and mentor other men. This man helps men deepen their spiritual maturity and build genuine friendships. They coordinate the discipleship training process, put together mentoring relationships and explore approaches for discipleship and spiritual formation.

5. **Ministry Projects and Resources.** This man leads the effort to find meaningful ministry for the men of the church. This man plans and coordinates community outreach and other short-term service-oriented projects. He is constantly looking for the best materials to win and disciple men such as our LifeBuilders Essentials discipleship course. He maintains a list of speakers, books, and other resources for the men, and makes these available at monthly meetings and other conferences.

Please don't hesitate to add positions to the leadership team.

LifeBuilders Leadership Team Chart

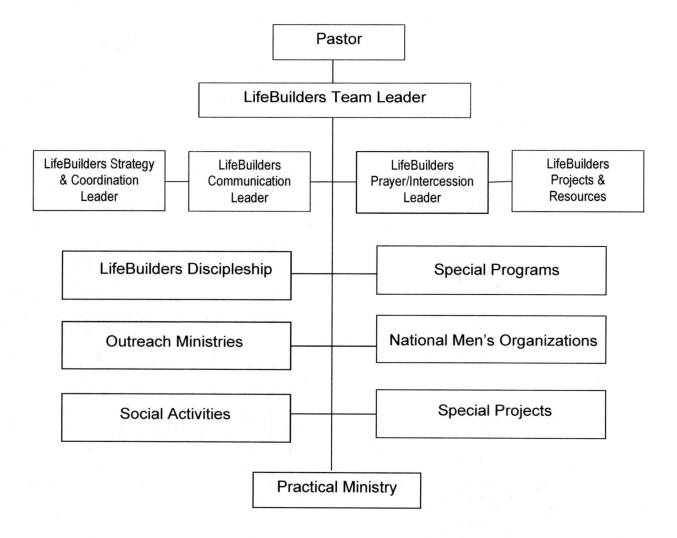

Train the LifeBuilders Leadership Team.

Leading the LifeBuilders Leadership Team in the discipleship process is vital to the long-term success of the ministry.

Train the team using this manual. LifeBuilders certified leaders will be provided certificates to present to team leaders who complete the training in the local church.

Lead the team through small group studies using the Transformational Discipleship Group Model. This model will strengthen relationships, develop missional leaders, and model effective small-group ministry that will be duplicated many times over. After the team leaders work through a small-group study you are now ready to launch small-group studies with other men in your men's group using the transformation group model.

Suggested studies:
- LifeBuilders Essentials
- James, a Path to Discipleship

Schedule a Leadership Team Kickoff Meeting

Now that you've got the men's leaders recruited and in place it's time to release them to lead. The ways in which these men are released become a model for the way they release others who will work under them. Always remember that the senior pastor or his appointee is always invited to be a part of this and any other gathering. Here are some pointers on the content of this meeting:

1. **Cast the vision.** Tell the leadership team exactly what should be accomplished through the LifeBuilders men's discipleship ministry chapter.

2. **State the purpose.** Why do we want a disciple-making ministry to the men of our church?

3. **Connect LifeBuilders to the church vision.** Show how this men's ministry moves men to support the vision and ministry of the church.

4. **Show the positive benefits of this effort**. Explain that the LifeBuilders men's ministry will not segregate the men, but instead motivate and empower them for leadership and service churchwide.

5. **Explain the commitment.** Tell the men what you expect from them. Clarify the amount of time and money necessary to get the job done right.

Start monthly LifeBuilders Meetings.

The regular meeting is important as part of building a "sustainable" men's ministry. By having a regular meeting, the momentum of the chapter is energized. It's also important for fellowship purposes and getting feedback for ministry improvement.

By "regular" meetings we mean monthly meetings. Failure to meet consistently makes the momentum difficult to sustain.

A Purposeful Meeting

Although it's periodic, that doesn't mean that the men meet just for the sake of getting together. If it does not speak to a specific need of the men, it could spell trouble for future involvement of proposed ministries.

It must be remembered that Christ is the model for every Christian man; therefore, the regular meetings must always be designed with the idea of building up men spiritually. Be creative.

A primary goal of a men's discipleship ministry is to involve every man in a discipleship process and meaningful ministry. The secret of a successful men's ministry is a variety of programs that will involve all the men. God is not looking for better programs; rather, He wants to build men for His kingdom. He puts His Spirit on men, not machinery. Every meeting should be spiritually meaningful and Christ-centered, with the goal of helping men grow spiritually and find their place of service in the church.

When we say every meeting must be spiritually meaningful, we are not referring to a business meeting or a regular event. We realize there will be meetings and events where the spiritual emphasis seems to be diminished, if not totally absent. Opportunities, such as sports events, work days, special trips, etc., provide the format for developing respect for and understanding of one another; and in doing so, have a team-building effect that will show itself in the spiritual character of the individual as well as the group. These are also opportunities to invite men to come to other events which address spiritual and personal issues more directly.

Establish a Pastor's Prayer Partner Ministry
The *Pastor's Prayer Partner* guide is in Section 9 of this manual.

Train Transformation Small Group Teachers
The *Transformational Discipleship Group Program* is in Section 8 of this manual.

LifeBuilders Checkup

(This form is to help determine the progress of your LifeBuilders ministry and identify specific actions for improvement and growth).

1. Do you have the support of the pastor?

2. Do you have a clear mission and vision?

3. Has your LifeBuilders leader received Level 2 Leadership Training?

4. Has your LifeBuilders team been selected?

5. Has your LifeBuilders leadership team received at least Level I Training?

6. Are your LifeBuilders leadership team members involved in a Transformational Small Group?

7. Have you had your kickoff meeting?

8. Is your LifeBuilders ministry chartered?

9. Have you selected and trained your small group leaders?

10. Do you have monthly LifeBuilders meetings?

11. Have you launched Transformational Small Groups?

12. Does your Pastor's Prayer Partner Ministry function consistently?

13. Do you communicate well (email, brochures, website, text messages, newsletters, or other ways)?

14. Do you have special days or big events to provide entry points for men into LifeBuilders Ministry?

15. What percentage of the men of your church are involved in Transformational Small Groups?

16. Do you celebrate your victories?

Get Men Involved In Ministries

It is frustrating for men to sit and watch. Men need to be involved in the life and ministries of the church. It is not enough to get men excited about ministry. We must give them opportunities.

This manual does not include all of the opportunities that are available for men. Your discipleship plan should not be confined to these ministries. There are many ministry opportunities available in your particular area that are unique to your location. Opportunities available in large metropolitan areas are not the same as those which present themselves in rural areas. Allow God to help you see and take advantage of new ministry opportunities.

SECTION 4

Planning the Program and Building Momentum

Step One – Meet with your pastor to discuss ways LifeBuilders can support him and build momentum for the church and LifeBuilders discipleship ministry. LifeBuilders is not about segregating men from women. LifeBuilders is about making disciples who participate in the full life and mission of the church. Discuss opportunities for LifeBuilders men to connect with new men and provide entry points into the LifeBuilders ministry.

Share the Pastor's Prayer Partner ministry with your pastor and develop it to fit the church and to be most effective for your pastor.

Discuss ways LifeBuilders men can bless the church and have fruitful discipleship ministry. Remember, RELATIONSHIPS are key to the discipleship process. The church schedule provides many opportunities to develop relationships and engage men in discipleship ministry. Here are a few:

1. Altar Services – LifeBuilders leaders and men should be trained to minister in the altar service. Praying with a man to be saved opens the door to bring him into the LifeBuilders group. Praying with men to be filled with the Holy Spirit, about a family problem, for healing, or another issue builds a spiritual bond between men that is necessary for the discipleship process. *Ministering at the Altar*, coauthored by Leonard Albert and Don Warrington is an excellent resource for this purpose.

   The members of a local congregation have a responsibility as spiritual leaders. As altar workers they can minister in a unique way. It is at the altar that lives are changed, needs are met, and burdens are lifted. We propose that twice annually, the local church teach a course in effective altar work. The goal is to organize a dedicated team of trained men who will be on hand during all the altar services at a local church.

2. Baby Dedication provides opportunities for LifeBuilders men to connect with new fathers. New fathers are always searching and desiring to become great dads. LifeBuilders provides the vehicle to help new dads grow in the Lord and in their skills as a dad. LifeBuilders is the perfect opportunity for the mentoring relationship to develop.

3. Every worship service is an opportunity for LifeBuilders men to get acquainted with men who are not in the discipleship process. Experience teaches us that relationship always comes before discipleship. Transformational Discipleship groups will help provide training and insight to outreach through the emphasis on reaching the lost, prayer for the lost and the Top Ten Card.

4. Weddings are a great time for LifeBuilders men to build relationships with men who are at a transition point in their lives.

5. The outreach of LifeBuilders men during the time of bereavement can be powerful. Teach LifeBuilders men the power of presence. By that I mean they don't need to try to speak words of comfort but rather allow the presence of the Holy Spirit in their lives to speak to the hurting person by just being there.

6. Workdays are always opportunities to connect with men. Men are looking for a way to fit into the life of the church. Workdays say, we need you but truthfully, the most important part of the workday is that relationships are built.

7. Softball, fishing tournaments, golf tournaments, and other activities draw men. One church did a Barbeque Cook Off; another church did a Wild Game Supper—great results with lots of men. These are events that give you the opportunity to introduce new men to LifeBuilders ministry.

8. Community outreach events.

9. Have cards made with a personal invitation to a special event. Give each man one card to give to another man to participate in the event.

10. Resurrection Breakfast. Details below:

What is Resurrection Breakfast?

Would you like to . . .
- Help men build relationships with unsaved friends?
- Add new life to your men's program?
- Involve men in evangelism?
- Get local churches active in ministry?
- See scores of unchurched men make a first-time commitment to Christ?

Your Answer: The Resurrection Breakfast!

The Resurrection Breakfast is an annual soulwinning event held in cities across America on the Saturday morning before Easter Sunday. This event is designed to challenge Christian men from all Evangelical denominations to form a citywide effort to invite other unsaved men to attend a breakfast and to hear a special speaker with a powerful testimony.

Easter is a season that presents a unique opportunity to reach men for Christ. Hearts are normally more tender and open at this time. If properly organized, the Resurrection Breakfast will involve your men in an unprecedented outreach to the community. Through this method you will reach men that heretofore would not respond to a church function.

Hundreds of breakfasts have been sponsored in cities across America, Canada, the Bahamas and in other countries. The speakers have included local civic, business, and sports figures; Christian judges, governors, and other elected officials; Christian movie and TV personalities; coaches; or anyone else who might have the name recognition to draw a crowd and present a soulwinning testimony. The results have been outstanding thousands of men have received Christ as their personal Savior.

We have witnessed firsthand what God has done through Resurrection Breakfasts. Church growth has occurred during the follow-up phase of these meetings. When men accept Christ at the breakfast, cards are filled out and distributed to area pastors who can then contact the new Christians to bring them into the church and disciple them.

Resurrection Breakfasts are held simultaneously in cities and communities around the world. Easter is natural time to reach new men and men who seldom attend church. It is essential to partner with the pastor and pastoral staff for followup. Resurrection Breakfast is a successful ministry program for reaching men during the Easter season.

The complete *Resurrection Breakfast Planning Guide* is in Section 10 of this manual.

Mission Teams

Discover the interest and skills of your men and plan mission teams directed toward their interest utilizing their skills. Ideas:

> Develop a Men of Action Team to provide assistance to retired people, widows, and others needing assistance. Winterizing homes, yard work, grocery shopping can all be difficult tasks. Completing these tasks helps the recipients, but also engages men in the mission.

> Develop short-term mission teams to travel and complete mission projects. Your team will bless the places they travel to and will also bless the team members.

Prayer Ministries

A regular time for Men's Prayer Ministry should be one of the top priorities of LifeBuilders. When men get together to pray, God moves to answer their prayers but God changes people who pray. People grow in the Lord when they pray. Start a weekly prayer meeting. Encourage your men to pray daily.

Major Events

Plan two major events each year to draw new men. These are cultural and community events that create an increase in attendance of at least 50 percent for the event. Follow-up and connectivity are essential for each event.

Ushers and Greeters Ministry

The purpose of the Ushers and Greeters is to utilize the talents of Christian men to promote a friendly welcome to every newcomer to the church service. This is a great way to get men involved, make visitors feel welcome and open the door of relationships with new men.

Men of Legacy

The Men of Legacy Program is designed for LifeBuilders men to intentionally develop relationships with young men and boys in order to leave a legacy of Christian faith and obedience to Christ. During the 2014-2016 General Assembly period, The Men of Legacy Program will use three initiatives to fulfill the mission:

> Christian Men's Fathering Initiative – Launch, January, 2015
> Devoted, Family Discipleship Initiative – Launch, May – June, 2015 (Pilot 2014)
> Royal Ranger Partnership with LifeBuilders Men – Launch, September (2015)

LifeBuilders Enlistment Week

The basic principle of LifeBuilders Discipleship Ministry is cooperation and service. The aim is to provide full cooperation with the pastor to partner with him/her in ministry. LifeBuilders enlistment week is a once-per-year emphasis where the local LifeBuilders group attempts to (1) enlist new members, (2) activate some who have not been regular in attendance, and (3) help start another LifeBuilders ministry in a nearby church.

LifeBuilders Recognition Sunday

Because men are responding in great numbers to the call of ministry, it is a good idea to set aside time for recognizing the efforts extended by them. We are seeing involvement in personal witness, prayer events, missions, mission projects as well as community projects.

It is appropriate to give special recognition to those who are working for the Kingdom among us. We can encourage and inspire more men to become involved in ministry by setting aside a special day or week to honor them and emphasize their value to the Christian cause.

We would advise you not to undertake this venture in a haphazard manner. If you are going to single out the workers, please do it prayerfully and in a manner which minimizes the chance of overlooking someone. It is extremely hard to go back and try to undo the damage a simple oversight may cause.

This special day has two purposes:

- To give special recognition to members who have contributed outstanding leadership, ministry, involvement, and spiritual awareness to the church

- To honor and recognize all men and emphasize their importance of a place for every man and a man for every place.

Pastor Appreciation Day

LifeBuilders Ministries are called upon to lead the way in honoring and blessing the pastor annually through Pastor Appreciation emphasis. Complete promotional resources, ideas, and gifts are available through www.coglifebuilders.com

Here are several reasons to honor your pastor on Pastor Appreciation Day:

- The Word of God teaches us to give honor to whom honor is due (1 Timothy 5:17). Elders who direct the affairs of the church well are worthy of double honor, especially those whose work is teaching and preaching.
- Pastors have a great responsibility to help believers discover God's plan for their life, and to grow to become mature believers faithfully fulfilling their divine purpose in the Kingdom.
- Appreciation and affirmation are great blessings to a pastor and his/her family in this high stress occupation. Satan goes about "as a roaring lion seeking whom he may devour" (1 Peter 5:8). The pastor and his/her family are primary targets. The enemy knows that striking the shepherd is a blow against the entire congregation. Consider these statistics:
  - 1,500 pastors leave the ministry permanently each month in America.
  - 80 percent of pastors and 85 percent of their spouses feel discouraged in their roles.
  - 71 percent of pastors say they are burned out, and they battle depression beyond fatigue on a weekly and even daily basis.
  - Only one out of every 10 ministers will actually retire as a minister.
- Your pastor is a gift to the church who shepherds the flock of God. This means that he/she feeds, protects, leads, and provides care for the flock.

Pastor Appreciation Day is an annual event designed to honor the local pastor and to focus attention on his biblical office. Your pastor is a special person—he/she is a leader, a spiritual guide, a partner in discipleship, and a friend. Although you appreciate your pastor every day of the year, it is fitting to set aside a day to honor the pastor publicly. This shows those outside the church the respect you have for the office of pastor.

Planning a successful Pastor Appreciation program does not have to be a burden. In fact, planning and total church participation are the keys to making it a great day. Form a committee, divide up the work, start early, and you will have a relaxed and memorable event. A lot of time, thought, and development have gone into producing a good variety of expressions of appreciation. Please visit the Pastor Appreciation page at www.coglifebuilders.com to find everything you will need to assist you in expressing your appreciation to your pastor.

Father's Day Promotion

Each local church LifeBuilders Men's Ministry group is encouraged to honor all dads each Father's Day. Visit www.coglifebuilders.com for low-cost gifts for dad each year.

As a part of the Father's Day emphasis, every family in the Church of God is invited to participate in family worship time, once each week for five weeks, beginning on Mother's Day and ending on Father's day. This special time is called DEVOTED: A Family Discipleship Initiative. More details are in Section 6.

SECTION 5

Conferences and Training Opportunities

LifeBuilders Leadership Training Conference
LifeBuilders Leadership Certification Conference
LifeBuilders Roundtable Sessions
LifeBuilders Men of Legacy Conference
LifeBuilders Rallies
Marriage and Family Retreats
Elders Training

LifeBuilders Leadership Training Conference

The LifeBuilders Leadership Training Conference is designed to:
- Help leaders understand the process of making disciples.
- Discover how to build and maintain effective discipleship ministry for men.
- Develop an outreach strategy for men.
- Develop leaders in men's discipleship.

LifeBuilders Leadership Certification Conference

Designed to train the men's leader to implement and maintain a successful men's ministry in the local church. Those completing the certification requirements may teach and certify local church team leaders.

LifeBuilders Leadership Roundtable Conference

The LifeBuilders Leadership Roundtables Conference is designed to train LifeBuilders Leadership Teams to rescue and disciple men. The conference addresses four areas:

1. The Problem – The Battle for Men's Souls

2. How to Build a LifeBuilders Leadership Team

3. How to Reach Men at the Heart Level

4. How to Disciple Men

The conference is informative and highly interactive. Men will work together in teams around tables to develop a strategic plan to win and disciple men in their church and community.

This conference meets the criteria for LifeBuilders Leadership Certification Training Level 1.

Men on a Mission

Men on a Mission is LifeBuilders ministry to missions. Specific projects will be selected according to need. Men will be recruited, trained, organized, and travel to the mission field to complete the needed mission. (Project Examples: discipleship training, evangelism, building and repair projects, crisis response, and other needs that might arise). This ministry is conducted as a partnership with World Missions, Men of Action, Chaplains Commission, and Mission States.

It is recommended that LifeBuilders Men on a Mission leaders travel with the team and serve with the leadership to learn and develop the necessary skills to lead men on the mission.

LifeBuilders Men of Legacy Conference

The LifeBuilders Men of Legacy Conference is designed to train and equip men to be better Christian witnesses, better husbands, and fathers, and better men for God. This is a meeting for men! The moral fiber of our society is weak. Where are the men of God? The LifeBuilders Men of Legacy Conferences are designed to confront men with the truth of God's Word and help them encounter the presence of God for forgiveness and deliverance. Men will be motivated and trained for leadership. They will discover:

- How to be a better husband and father.
- How to understand the unique problems of Christian manhood.
- How to connect and minister in LifeBuilders men's discipleship in the local church.
- How to find their place of ministry in God's plan.

LifeBuilders Rallies

A worship service designed to lead men to an encounter with Jesus Christ at the altar.

Fellowship Meals

There were many times in God's Word when people came together to share a meal. A real highlight in the social activities of a men's or women's group is a frequent fellowship meal. By inviting good guest speakers, the time can be informative, inspirational and a time of connecting. Recent church visitors, unsaved people, and newcomers to the community can all be invited to attend.

Elders Training

The *Ministry of Elders Manual* is designed to assist in implementing Elders Ministry in the local church. A *Ministry of Elders Manual* is included in the Section 14 in this manual.

Pastor's Prayer Partners

The monthly meeting is a good place to launch the Pastor's Prayer Partner Program. The program is included in Section 9 of this manual.

SECTION 6

DEVOTED Family Discipleship Initiative

Every family in the Church of God is invited to participate in family worship time, once each week for five weeks, beginning on Mother's Day and ending on Father's Day.

Our Mission

1. Help families develop the habit of family worship/discipleship time together.

2. Help families make family discipleship a lifestyle.

3. Support family revival and healing.

4. Challenge every family member to be a disciple of Jesus Christ making disciples.

5. Raise up godly men and women who will raise their families with the commitment, "As for me and my house, we will serve the Lord.

6. Provide an opportunity for fathers, mothers and heads of households to have a fresh beginning as spiritual leaders.

7. To support foundational theological beliefs.

A resource webpage will be provided for participating churches to download resources, upload videos, and give input.

SECTION 7

LifeBuilders Discipleship Training

(For every man in your men's group.)

Discipleship 100

Those completing seven books in the Discipleship 100 series will receive a Certificate of Recognition. Certificates will be provided from the International LifeBuilders Men's Discipleship office. We recommend that men who complete the 100 series be recognized in a special LifeBuilders Celebration Service

- *LifeBuilders Essentials*
- *James, A Path to Discipleship*
- *Philippians, A Path to Joy*
- *Maximized Manhood*
- *Courage*
- *Wild at Heart*
- *Real Man*
- *Praying The Breath of Life*

Discipleship 200

Those completing seven books in the Discipleship 200 series will receive a Certificate of Commission. Certificates will be provided from the International LifeBuilders Men's Discipleship office. We recommend that men who complete the 200 series be recognized in a special LifeBuilders Commissioning Service.

- *Never Quit*
- *Sexual Integrity*
- *Daring*
- *The Power of Potential*
- *Treasure*
- *Communication, Sex and Money*
- *Strong Men in Tough Times*

Discipleship 300

Discipleship 300 is Ministry/Leadership Training available through partnership of LifeBuilders with other Church of God Ministries; and completing the following books. A Certificate of Service will be provided from the International LifeBuilders Men's Discipleship office. We recommend that men who complete the 300 series be recognized in a special LifeBuilders recognition service.

- *Sleeping Giants*
- *How God Makes Men*
- *Man Alive*
- *Characters With Character*

Men on a Mission

Men on a Mission is LifeBuilders ministry to missions. Specific projects will be selected according to need. Men will be recruited, trained, organized, and travel to the mission field to complete the needed mission. (Project Examples: discipleship training, evangelism, building and repair projects, crisis response, and other needs that might arise). This ministry is conducted as a partnership with World Missions, Men of Action, Chaplaincy Commission, and Mission States.

It is recommended that LifeBuilders Men on a Mission leaders travel with the team and serve with the leadership to learn and develop the necessary skills to lead men on future mission projects.

Certificate in Ministerial Studies (CIMS)

About the Program:

Those called to the ministry after their formal education has been completed often find that the opportunity to attend a college or seminary requires financial responsibilities that are difficult to meet, especially with a family. With the understanding that ministerial training is needed, the church has instituted the Certificate In Ministerial Studies (CIMS), a nontraditional training curriculum, that provides an opportunity for every minister to receive ministerial training in a Distance Learning Center or via personal or Internet study.

The Certificate in Ministerial Studies (CIMS) consists of 20 courses, offering 35 credits. Of the 35 credits, 34 are required for the CIMS certificate. While CIMS is open to any qualified applicant, the program was designed for ministers who hold Church of God credentials or who have been set forth for ministry by a local church.

About online studies:

The Certificate in Ministerial Studies program may be completed online over your home computer at your convenience.

These dynamic studies include some of the most advanced Internet technology available such as streaming video, audio, and text.

For additional information visit www.ministerialtraining.org

Community Service Chaplains

The International Association of Community Service Chaplains offers a 3-day intensive course in Community Service Chaplaincy. This training experience will prepare the student to be an effective and skilled Community Service Chaplain, better able to care for people "beyond the gates" of the local church who are hurting, lonely, in crisis, or destitute. The class instructional process and format will include a variety of visual aids, role-play scenarios, small/large group work/discussion, and instruction with class dialogue. The purpose of this training is to provide students with an understanding of key issues, concepts, and skills necessary to facilitate effective community ministry and empower the local church pastor and lay leadership to really care for others by reaching out to hurting humanity in the church and local community. There are a large variety of topics taught during this 3-day seminar. The topics are designed to be applied immediately to ministry, both inside the church and in the marketplace.

Many Community Service Chaplains respond to disasters across the U.S.A. on a regular basis. More information may be obtained at www.tiacsc.com

Mobilize: Local Leadership Development

For more information visit www.cogdoe.org/mobilize-local-leadership-development.html

LLD has been very successful in training local church leaders. Throughout the years, pastors who have used LLD have given glowing testimonies about how effective the ministry has been for training their leaders.

Mobilize is a 12-month program that assists the local church pastor to motivate, equip, and train leaders for the local congregation.

Level I includes pastor-supervised, independent Bible study and readings in leadership, monthly seminars led by the pastor, and ministry assignments within the local congregation. Level 2 is pastor-supervised, independent Bible study and training in one of 11 areas of local church ministry.

Discipleship 400

Discipleship 400 is Ministry/Leadership Training available through partnership of LifeBuilders with other Church of God Ministries.

Operation Compassion

Additional information and contact can be made at www.operationalcompassion.org

Mission Statement

Operation Compassion focuses on three priorities: (1) responding to natural disasters nationally and around the world; (2) providing inspiration, information, training and resources to help mobilize churches, individuals and community groups to provide food and basic necessities to the poor and needy; (3) concentrating on international distribution to widows, single mothers and children.

Key Programs

- **Relief America: The Disaster Response Network** Responding to national and international natural disasters with containers of bottled water, food, cleaning supplies, building materials, etc.; establishing an in-country local network of churches, agencies, and government leaders to meet the needs of children and families.
- **Compassion America: The Urban Network** Meeting various needs of the poor and underprivileged living within America's largest cities by utilizing partnerships with civic and community leaders, school districts, police departments, fire departments, parks and recreation departments, churches and other local agencies.
- **Dream America: The Native American Network** Supplying Native Americans living on reservations in the western United States with many necessities that are difficult to obtain, including food, water, educational material and building supplies; children and widows are a priority.
- **Hope America: The Appalachia Network** Targeting one of the four most extreme areas of poverty in the U.S. through food distribution, hot meals, job training and home repair; focusing on children, single parents, widows and senior adults.
- **Global Compassion Network** Providing countries of the developing world with medical supplies, medical equipment, textbooks, clothing, food, and toys; targeting children, widows, and senior adults.

Men of Action

The Men of Action mission is to provide men and women with the opportunity to show the love of Christ by participating in hands-on ministry through volunteer services in construction, disaster relief, and humanitarian assistance around the world while enhancing other ministries so they will be more effective, efficient, and fruitful in their participation in the Great Commission.

For more information and current projects visit www.cogmwoa.org

SECTION 8

Transformational LifeBuilders Discipleship Groups

David H. Gosnell, D.Min.
Men's Discipleship Coordinator

Transformational Discipleship Groups
Making the Most of Your Time Together

DEVELOP THE GROUP THROUGH INVITATION

Select four or at most five men to be in your group. Include at least one mature believer and at least one new believer. Your goal is clear: Lead every member of the group to grow in Jesus Christ to discover and fulfill God's personal call on their life. This is a transformation group where every member will grow and be fully involved in the discipleship process personally and leading others in the discipleship process.

ENCOURAGE THE USE OF THE MATERIAL

It is important for each man to have his personal study book. We believe that having the group members read, and collect their thoughts for each of the lessons will vastly improve your group experience and is key to getting the most out of this study. While group time is important, the reading and preparation each member does prior to the meeting is more personal and will challenge each group member to go deeper.

PROVIDE A WELCOME SETTING

Be creative. Arrange the seating so that everyone can face one another (Example: around a table). This creates an atmosphere where everyone feels part of the discussion. Avoid theatre style seating. After the discussion, you might want to have coffee available so that those who want to talk personally will feel more comfortable and will be more likely to do so. And be careful to let others help you clean up if they volunteer. It'll make them feel like they're a part of things, so if they ask to help, accept it!

DICSIPLESHIP GROUP MEETING FORMAT

We realize that small groups come in all shapes and sizes. They are hosted in a variety of venues and settings and have varying time constraints. As the leader, you will need to take these factors into account and structure your group time accordingly. So, we created the study materials so that you can customize your meetings to fit your particular needs.

Recommended Format

- Fellowship/Testimonies/Stories

- Opening Prayer

- Discuss – reaching the lost objectives

    - (Identify and pray for lost people weekly. Use Top Ten Card.)

- Discuss the weekly lesson material

- Praise & Prayer Requests

- Prayer Time (10 minutes)

Steps to Leading a Life Changing Small Group

1. Get to know group members.

2. Get everyone participating.

    A. Discipleship is not lecturing.

    B. Have expectation that everyone participates.

    C. Ask questions.

    D. Make it fulfilling so they want to return.

    E. Reduce and eliminate embarrassing and threatening situations.

    F. Protect and honor confidentiality.

3. The Mechanics

    A. Content - God's Word

    B. Care

    C. Commitment & accountability

    D. Consistency/continuity - set the example

E. Carefully prepare - demonstrate and subscribe value to study

F. Composition - study, prayer, fellowship and accountability

4. Accountability/stewardship

A. Care so much you won't accept poor decisions or justification. Keep antennas up.

B. Don't be judgmental!

C. Pray over group.

D. Be a mentor/disciple maker.

E. Be yourself. Be real. Be holy. Be humble.

F. Trust God.

Finally, we also want to give you a heads up that you may not get through all the questions each week. That's okay. The important thing is that your group is really engaging with the material, and wrestling with it on a personal level. If you find yourself running out of time on more than one occasion, you'll likely want to read through the questions ahead of your next meeting, and prioritize the ones you feel are most important. Resist the temptation to run over. Respect everyone's time and you'll have a group eager to return for the next session.

THE FIRST MEETING

At the first meeting of your discipleship group, open the meeting with prayer and then have the members introduce themselves and share about their families, their spiritual lives, and other personal information.

You should have a **covenant signing ceremony** at the first meeting (see separate document). In each other's presence you sign the covenant as an open demonstration of everyone's commitment to keep the covenant and as an invitation to be held accountable to it by each other.

Finally, review the discipleship curriculum. Share an overview of the table of contents and the layout of one of the lessons so that the member gets a sense for what is involved. We would also stress the fact that discipling is not about completing a lesson in a workbook. The curriculum is a tool that provides some structure for the relationship. *Tools do not make disciples. The Lord uses people to make disciples.*

Close the session with prayer.

The Weekly Meeting

You should use the first 10 minutes for fellowship and personal sharing about what is happening in each other's lives; then have one of the members, or you open with prayer.

The next 15 minutes are to be given to talking about lost people who are in your lives and praying for them by name. If they don't have friendships with lost people, time should be spent talking and praying about how they can connect with people who are not church goers. Use the Top Ten Card. Every man should have a Top Ten Card with names of people he is praying for daily to be saved. You might have an empty chair in the room representing the people whose names are on the cards. Pray for those cards weekly.

They next 45 minutes are spent on the responses to the questions in the material that each man has previously prepared. Go at a pace that seems comfortable to the group and is not so regimented that it does not allow time to chase rabbit trails. You want to encourage participants to introduce questions that are prompted from the study. It is also important not to rush the personal application to the various dimensions of one's life.

You should fully participate in the discussions with your insights as one of the participating members of the group. You should be transparent. It is important that you share your personal struggles, prayer concerns, and confession of sin. The group will probably go as deep personally as, or take risks to the extent that, they see the leader doing. Trust develops incrementally. The degree of self-revelation will need to be matched to the level of trust that has been developed.

Use the final 10 minutes to share praises and prayer requests followed by praying for the needs of the group.

Group Facilitator's Role

As the group leader, you have the opportunity to play an important part in sharing a message that has the power to transform lives. But please understand, your primary role is that of a friend and a servant. It is not the leader's job to judge someone else's status. It is the leader's job to provide a safe place where participants can honestly explore their relationship with Jesus. It is the leader's job to model Jesus by being genuinely concerned about the thoughts, questions, and struggles of the group members.

As the leader, you don't need any special training or leadership experience to host a group. You don't have to be a teacher—in fact, it's better if the leader doesn't teach. All you have to do is facilitate the conversation, keep the discussion moving and make sure the atmosphere is open, non-judgmental, and conversational. Take the journey yourself; be frank and honest with our group as you share the things that God is revealing to you along the way, and be as open to learning from the group as you are committed to serving them as their leader. I'm sure that if you approach the study with that kind of open heart and humble spirit, your group members won't be the only ones who are blessed.

Tips for Guiding Discussion

Since one of your primary responsibilities is to keep the conversation going, we've included some really important tips for you to consider. Guiding the discussion is important to your group's success. Please, don't skip over this; make sure you really digest these concepts. And then go over these tips with other group members and ask them to give you their feedback after the discussion time.

Pray

Ask God to give you wisdom, a listening ear, and a peace that passes understanding. 2 Timothy 1:7 says that we should pray for a spirit of power, of love, and of self-discipline.

Ask Questions

The study guides contains questions that lead the conversation to a discipleship process. Feel free to rephrase the questions to make them your own. The more conversational you can be, the better. The real key is to not just ask one question right after another, but to follow up with what someone says. This makes the discussion more like a conversation than a lesson. So, here are some good follow-up questions to have in your back pocket: "Explain what you mean." Or you might ask, "Can you give an example of what you're saying?" Or "When did you start thinking or feeling that way?" Or "How confident are you that that's true?" Or "How well does that work in your life?" Maybe you say, "Well that's interesting. What do the rest of you think?"

Listen

Keep in mind that the most important thing you need to do next is LISTEN! Really hear what people are saying. Don't worry so much about what you're going to say next. Instead, really listen, and then respond out of what you hear people say. You'll also want to be careful to talk enough but not talk too much. A little silence can be a good thing for a group; so don't try to fill every quiet moment. Do your best to listen to the Holy Spirit as well as the conversation. Be praying silently all through the discussion time, asking for the sensitivity and wisdom to listen and then guide without controlling.

Your Opinion

Another important key is to be sure not to give your opinion about an issue unless it has already been fully discussed. Some people will see you as the leader and once you speak they'll shut down. So, if someone asks for your opinion you might say. "I'll be glad to give it, but let's hear from everyone else first."

Affirm vs. Endorse

It's important that, as a leader, you affirm all the responses. You say, "Thank you Ben." Or "That's very interesting, Greg." Not matter what the participants say, don't criticize their remarks. What they just said may be antagonistic to you, it may be stupid, it may simply sound ridiculous, but don't directly criticize it. Instead say something like, "Well that's interesting. What do the rest of you think?" Once, you as the leader directly disapprove of someone's comments, then some people will never speak up again. They're going to fear disapproval. And once exploration stops for them, then the journey does too. But on the other side of the coin, while it's important to affirm all responses, avoid the temptation to endorse them. Don't say things like "Now that's a great comment" or "I couldn't agree with you more." Such endorsements tip your hand and leave others feeling like their comments are not acceptable. Also, resist the urge to be too instructional, trying to answer everyone's questions and solve everyone's problems. Once a know-it-all person speaks up, conversation tends to shut down. You can give your own opinion, but do it in a personal and humble way. Maybe you say, "Well my experience has been . . ." or "This is how I see it . . ."

When Someone Talks Too Much

What do you do if you have a difficult, or domineering, or excessively talkative person in your group? Here are a few ideas: First, if someone is talking on and on—interrupt nicely and say, "I see what you mean, I hear what you're trying to say, but let's see how others feel about that." Or another thing you might want to do is if someone is regularly talking too much, you might say, "I'd like to give everyone else a chance to say one thing before anyone speaks a second time." Also, if someone continues to just dominate the group or the discussion time, step aside with him or her after the session and say something like, "I see you have a lot of ideas, and you're very willing to express them. That's awesome, but I need your help. Some of the others in the group, they're not as bold. So, would you help me draw them out? If you could keep your comments a little briefer, not speak up quite as much. I think they're going to begin to share. So, if you could help me with that, it would be great."

When Someone Never Talks

What if you have a person in your group who never talks and they're reluctant to share? You might say something like, "Does anyone who hasn't spoken up yet have a thought or an idea." If that doesn't work, and if the Spirit is prompting you, then maybe you can say, "Hey, Kevin, I noticed you haven't said anything yet—you don't have to but I'd sure be interested in hearing what you think about this." We realize this may be a ton of information for you to digest (especially if you are a new leader), but don't worry. Above all, just love each person in the group because if you truly care about them, they're going to sense it, and then allow the Holy Spirit to do the rest.

Sample Top Ten Cards and Forms are available for download at: coglifebuilders.com/lifebuildersforms.htm.

Transformational Discipleship Groups
Covenant 1

<u>PRIORITY</u>: The group meeting will be a priority in my schedule. If I am running late or unable to attend, I will contact my group leader.

<u>PREPAREDNESS</u>: I realize that what I put into the lesson is what I will get out of it. Therefore, I will prepare for the lesson each week and come prepared to share.

<u>RESPECT</u>: Everyone has a right to their opinion and all questions are encouraged and respected. I will listen attentively to others without interrupting them.

<u>CONFIDENTIALITY</u>: Anything of a personal nature that is said in the meeting should not be repeated outside the meeting. This group is intended to be a safe place for open discussion and sharing.

<u>HONESTY</u>: I will strive to be real, honest, and transparent with the other group members.

<u>SUPPORT</u>: The mission and values of the group have my support and I will refrain from gossip or criticism.

<u>SIGNATURES</u>:   <u>DATE</u>: _____

_____

_____

_____

_____

_____

_____

Transformational Discipleship Groups
Covenant 2

In order to grow toward maturity in Christ and complete the discipleship material, I commit myself to the following standards:

1. Complete all assignments on a weekly basis prior to my groups meeting in order to contribute fully.

2. Meet weekly with my discipleship partners for approximately one and one-half hours to discuss the content of the assignments.

3. Offer myself fully to the Lord with the anticipation that I am entering a time of accelerated transformation during this discipleship period.

4. Contribute to a climate of honest, trust, confidentiality, and personal vulnerability in a spirit of mutual respect and encouragement.

5. Give serious consideration to continuing the discipleship chain by committing myself to invest in at least two other people for the year following the initial completion of the discipleship material.

SIGNATURES: DATE: _____

_____

_____

_____

_____

_____

_____

Top Ten

1.

2.

3.

4.

5.

6.

7.

8.

9.

10.

Top Ten

1.

2.

3.

4.

5.

6.

7.

8.

9.

10.

Top Ten

1.

2.

3.

4.

5.

6.

7.

8.

9.

10.

Top Ten

1.

2.

3.

4.

5.

6.

7.

8.

9.

10.

SECTION 9

PASTOR'S PRAYER PARTNERS

Acknowledgments

In honor of Pastor David Bishop
and appreciation to
the Westmore Church of God Prayer Partners
who supplied invaluable help
and served as a model for this project.

This book can be ordered from:

Church of God Men's Discipleship
www.coglifebuilders.com
888-766-9009

Pastor's Prayer Partners
Table of Contents

Pastor's Prayer Partners

Overview

A. What Is Pastor's Prayer Partners?

The Pastor's Prayer Partners program is designed to give interceding prayer support for the pastor and the ministries of the church. Those involved in this endeavor commit to pray for the:

- Pastor
- Pastoral staff
- Church family
- Church ministries

B. How Does This Ministry Function?

This ministry functions under the primary oversight of the pastor. In addition, a Prayer Partners Coordinator must be appointed to assist the pastor. The coordinator's responsibilities include the preparation of a monthly newsletter, periodic prayer breakfasts and the annual Prayer Partners Retreat. Also, a Prayer Captain is appointed for each week to direct the prayer time in the pastor's office.

Prayer Partners commit to the following schedule of prayer:

Consistent personal prayer

One Sunday each month when scheduled partners gather in the pastor's office for prayer

One week of intense prayer for the church each month (This week is the one prior to their scheduled Sunday prayer time.)

One day a month when each prayer partner prays especially for the pastor (This day is the same day each month throughout the year.)

During the Sunday prayer time in the pastor's office, Prayer Partners gather as a designated time to hear from the pastor as to the direction of ministry for the day and to learn of any special concerns needing prayer. Then the Prayer Partners lay hands on the pastor and ask God's anointing on him for the service. While the pastor conducts the morning worship, the Prayer Partners remain to intercede throughout the duration of the service. A Prayer agenda is prepared each Sunday to assist the partners in knowing the needs for the day. Prayer partners who are praying during the service may receive a free CD of the service from the media ministry desk.

C. Who May Be Involved in This Ministry?

The Pastor's Prayer Partners Ministry is open to members of the LifeBuilders Men's Discipleship Ministry and other men of the church. Participation is determined by an invitation from the pastor.

D. What Are the Requirements of This Ministry?

Prayer Partners make the following one-year agreements:

1. Prayer commitments as mentioned above.
2. Attend a maximum of four prayer breakfast meetings.
3. Attend the annual Prayer Partners Retreat.

II. Preliminary Steps

Discuss the Pastor's Prayer Partners program in a LifeBuilders Discipleship meeting or special called meeting of all interested men of the church. A sample form letter to announce such a meeting is on page 73.

Prior to the initial meeting the pastor should identify and get a commitment from a prayer coordinator. This should be a person with a heart for prayer ministry and who is willing to serve for a full year. His title will be "Prayer Partners Coordinator." The duties are defined in detail on page 67 of this document.

Once the men come together for the meeting, the pastor and prayer partners' coordinator should each have time to share with the group their personal burdens for the prayer ministry.

III. Organizational Meeting

A. Introduction

The disciples recognized the need for prayer so they asked Jesus to teach them to pray (Luke 11:1). That need has not diminished in today's society. We must again focus on the desire to pray and seek God's will in all that we do in faith believing He will supply the answers.

Matthew Henry once said, "When God purposes great grace for His people, He sets them to praying."

God's Word declares

> "Call unto me, and I will answer thee, and show thee great and mighty things, which thou knowest not" (Jeremiah 33:3).

> "And all things, whatsoever ye shall ask in prayer, believing, ye shall receive" (Matthew 21:22).

> "Therefore I say unto you, What things soever ye desire, when ye pray, believe that ye receive them, and ye shall have them" (Mark 11:24).

> "For with God nothing shall be impossible" (Luke 1:37).

> "If ye abide in me, and my words abide in you, ye shall ask what ye will, and it shall be done unto you" (John 15:7).

B. The Focus

1. Men must learn to pray as stated in God's Word for effective ministry in the local church

    a. Acknowledging the belief that God answers prayer.

    b. Understanding God wants to do more through answered prayer than we have dreamed possible.

2. Men need to meditate upon God and His Promises.

C. Mobilization of the Men for Prayer

1. Introduce the Pastor's Prayer Partners coordinator who was selected prior to the organizational meeting.

2. Discuss the following guidelines to which men must commit to be a prayer partner:

    a. A personal relationship with God and a desire to better serve Him

    b. A hunger to be a part of a focused prayer ministry

    c. A willingness to have a personal prayer relationship with the pastor who will be the first to know the . . .
    - burden
    - vision
    - need
    - results

    d. A commitment of one year to the Pastor's Prayer Partners ministry

D. How the Program Works

One day a month each prayer partner will make the pastoral ministries of the local church a focused matter of prayer. (Groups smaller than 31 in number may be assigned more than one day per month.) That day may coincide with the partner's birthday as a reminder to pray on that particular day. In any event, each person will pray especially one day a month. Only one person will be assigned to pray on a given day. All prayer partners are encouraged to pray for the pastor whenever they think to do so.

One Sunday morning each month, up to five men will be scheduled for special prayer. They will meet with the pastor in his office at a designated time. During this time, the pastor shares recent answers to prayer and briefs the men on the service as to the . . .
- focus
- special needs
- faith goals

The men should then lay hands on the pastor and pray for him. While the pastor leads the morning worship, the prayer partners pray together for the service.

The entire program working properly is dependent on the prayer coordinator and prayer captain faithfully performing their assigned duties. In addition it is extremely important that prayer helps be provided each Sunday. This advance preparation allows more time to be given to intercessory prayer.

1. Duties of the prayer coordinator:

    a. Notifies the men each month as to the week and Sunday each man will serve

    b. Assigns a prayer captain for each Sunday of the month

    c. Assists the pastor in providing prayer materials, outlines, etc., for each Sunday

    d. Helps the pastor in planning the quarterly prayer breakfast and annual retreat

    e. Serves as a contact person for the prayer partners in the event they have a conflict with the schedule

2. Duties of the Sunday prayer captain:

    a. Leads the prayer group on his assigned Sunday

    b. Keeps the prayer group focused on the theme for a given Sunday

    c. Introduces various methods of prayer and worship as needed to maintain the momentum of the group such as:

- related Bible reading
- singing
- individual and corporate prayer
- praying for specific needs

3. Provided prayer helps

a. The pastor may wish to share his sermon outline and prayer suggestions.

b. An outline of children's church activities and prayer requests should be provided.

c. A list of all prayer requests turned into the church office should be prepared by the church secretary.

d. Members of the prayer partners group will also share prayer requests.

e. Other prayer resources

E. Implementing a Plan for Continuing Prayer Enrichment

1. Prayer Breakfast

The entire prayer group will meet with the pastor four times a year (quarterly) for a prayer breakfast that will include:

a. Food & fellowship
b. Songs & worship
c. Reflection of the importance of prayer
d. Testimonies of answered prayer
e. Prayer for one another
f. Prayer for the pastor

2. Prayer Retreat (See pages 21-22 for sample retreat schedules.)

The entire prayer group will meet once a year for a Saturday Prayer Partners retreat that will include:

a. Food
b. Fellowship
c. Instruction
d. Prayer

F. Conclusion

The Pastor's Prayer Partners program is an exciting and challenging ministry opportunity because it makes prayer a top priority, enhances personal ministry, and creates an atmosphere in which God can bless. In addition it serves as a training ground for spiritual leadership for men.

Let us pray!

Illustration: Wilbur Chapman tells the story of going to Wanamakers Church as the new pastor. An old man came up to him and said, "You are a younger man than I expected. I am afraid you won't succeed so I am going to pray for you. In fact, I have two others who have agreed to covenant with me in prayer." From that humble beginning they saw the number of that group grow to 10, then 20, then 50, and then 219 who prayed for the pastor continually. In that environment it was easy to preach. In three years they had 1,000 conversions, 600 of whom were men.

How the Program Supports the Pastor Through Prayer (Ephesians 6:10-18)

Praying for the Pastor
"Be strong in the Lord and the strength of His might" **(Ephesians 6:10).**

Meditate   the greatness of God in behalf of your pastor (Romans 8:28, 31, 37; 1 Peter 3:12).

Expose   the wiles of the devil (Ephesians 6:11,12).

Claim   scriptural promises for his overall protection
(Isaiah 54:14-17; Psalm 34:7; Psalm 91; Luke 10:19; 1 Corinthians 10:3,4).

Petition   the Father to grant him a discerning spirit (2 Corinthians 11:14; 1 John 4:1).

The Pastor's Private Life
"Stand, therefore, girded in truth" **(Ephesians 6:14).**

Request   that his glory be solely in the Cross (Galatians 6:14).

Pray   for his continued renewal (Isaiah 40:27-31).
for true holiness (1 Peter 1:16).

Seek   for him a clear vision of the merits of Christ (Philippians 3:7-10).
for godly contentment (1 Timothy 6:6).
for the love of God to be shed abroad in his heart (Romans 5:5).

The Pastor's Personal Life
"Stand . . . having put on the breastplate of righteousness" **(Ephesians 6:14).**

Intercede   for his spouse, children and family (Psalm 37:25; Psalm 91:9-12).

Cancel   in Jesus' name all assignments against him (Matthew 16:19).

Remove   by faith all obstacles to his total health and prosperity (Mark 11:23; Philippians 4:19).

The Pastor's Praise Life
"Stand . . . having shod your feet with the equipment of the gospel of peace"
(Ephesians 6:15).

Ask   the Father to give him a strong worship (Matthew 4:10).

Bind   the spirit of fear (John 14:1).
the spirit of gloom (Isaiah 61:3).
the spirit of negativity (2 Timothy 1:6,7).
for any other direction (Ecclesiastes 5:1,2).

The Pastor's Prayer Life
"Stand . . . above all taking the shield of faith, with which you can quench all the flaming darts of the evil one" (Ephesians 6:16).

Quench   in the Holy Spirit all darts of doubt (Mark 6:5,6).

Rebuke   all distractions from his devotional time (Mark 5:36).

Loosen   the forces of heaven to aid him in prayer (Mark 1:35; Acts 1:14).

The Pastor's Professional Life
"Stand . . . taking the helmet of salvation" (Ephesians 6:17).

Shield   him from the fear of men (Proverbs 19:23; Isaiah 11:1-3).

Bestow   on him favor in the denomination (Proverbs 18:16).
support among his peers (Proverbs 11:4).

Entreat   Jesus to give him an uncompromising truth (Proverbs 4:20-27).
wisdom in leadership (James 1:5).

The Pastor's Preaching Life
"Stand . . .pray at all times in the spirit, with all prayer and supplication. To that end keep alert with all perseverance . . ."
(Ephesians 6:17).

Bless   him with rich study time (Acts 6:4; 2 Timothy 2:15).

Grant   to him a bold proclamation of Jesus (Colossians 1:28).
opportunities (Colossians 4:3,4).

Anoint   him to preach and teach (Luke 4:18; 1 John 2:27).
for apostolic results (Acts 2:37).
for signs and wonders (Mark 16:20).
to reveal truth (Matthew 16:17).

The Pastor's Persevering Life
"Stand . . . with the sword of the spirit, which is the word of God"
(Ephesians 6:16).

Honor   him with lasting fruit (Malachi 3:11; John 15:16).

Confess   steadfastness over him (1 Corinthians 15:58).
bold vision (Isaiah 41:10).
rest (Matthew 11:38; Hebrews 4).

Give   thanks for his call and gifts (Colossians 1:3-5).

Secure   him in courage (Joshua 1).

"Fight the good fight of faith"
(1 Timothy 6:12).

Expect   all that you have prayer.

Stand   behind him, girding him in prayer

Yield   to the Spirit for other areas of prayer and intercession.

Amen

Renewal Ministries, Inc., P.O. Box 8254, College Station, TX 77842. Used by permission.

Role of a Pastor's Prayer Partner

Who is a Pastor's Prayer Partner?
- ✔ A godly layman willing to commit valuable time and energy to an organized sustained prayer program for the pastor.

What kind of person does it take?
- ✔ A person who is committed to God and desires to serve Him.

- ✔ A person who desires to be a part of a fervent prayer ministry.

- ✔ A person who is willing to have a personal prayer relationship with the pastor.

- ✔ A person who is faithful for the duration of the Prayer Partners Ministry.

What are the specific duties performed?
- ✔ Pray for the pastor and church one day each month.

- ✔ Pray with the pastor one Sunday each month.

- ✔ Attend the scheduled prayer breakfasts.

- ✔ Attend the annual Pastor's Prayer Partners retreat.

What results are expected?
- ✔ Make prayer a top priority.

- ✔ Enhance personal ministry.

- ✔ Serve as a training ground for spiritual leadership.

- ✔ Create an atmosphere in which God can bless.

Sample Letter to Potential
Pastor's Prayer Partners

(date)

(name and address)

Dear   :

The purpose of my letter is to invite you to consider becoming a part of what we are calling the **Pastor's Prayer Partners** ministry. We are praying for 31 men to respond—a person for every day of the month. You are one of the 31 prospects to whom we are sending letters. We are asking for a one-year commitment.

The following is a list of the expectations we have in mind.

1. Pray in the conference room and/or pastor's office one morning service per month.

2. Join with me and the other Prayer Partners four times a year for breakfast, a lesson, and time of prayer together.

3. Commit to pray for the pastoral staff and ministry of our church on a consistent and regular basis.

4. Be open to personal prayer ministry in your life.

After prayerful consideration, please fill out the enclosed slip and return it to me at your earliest convenience. On Sunday, (date) at (time), we will have an orientation meeting at which time you may ask questions and make a final decision.

There is a special bonding in relationships through prayer. I would love to have the opportunity of being a prayer partner with you. I need you!

Laborers together in Christ,

(name of pastor)
Enclosure

Enclosure With Initial Letter to Potential Pastor's Prayer Partners
PASTOR'S PRAYER PARTNERS
(name of Church)
RESPONSE FORM

NAME _____

ADDRESS _____

_____

PHONE _____

E-MAIL _____

☐ I am willing to commit to participate in the Pastor's Prayer Partners program this year.

☐ I regret that I will not be able to participate in the pastor's Prayer Partners program this year.

I would like to recommend the names listed below as possible candidates for participation in the Pastor's Prayer Partners program:

_____

_____

_____

_____

Sample Pastor's Prayer Partners
Acknowledgment Letter

(date)

(name and address)

Dear (name):

My heart was warmed to receive the response form with your signature saying you would be meeting with us on Sunday, (date) at (time), to learn more of about the **Pastor's Prayer Partners** ministry. The meeting will be held in (location). At that time we will be sharing with you the plans and scope of what is being envisioned for this ministry.

I am excited! Matthew Henry once said, "When God intends great grace for His people, He sets them to praying." I believe we are sensing such a nudge of the Spirit. In addition, I believe (your city) is poised for spiritual breakthrough, and it is my desire that (name of your church) be on the cutting edge of what God is going to do.

Thank you for your interest. I shall be looking forward to seeing you on (date).

God bless you!

Yours in Christ,

(name of pastor)

Enclosure (organizational meeting program)

PASTOR'S PRAYER PARTNERS

Organizational Meeting

(date)

Welcome .... *(pastor)*

Introductions .... *(pastor)*

Purpose of Pastor's Prayer Partners Ministry........................*(prayer coordinator)*

Overview of the Ministry .... *(pastor)*

Questions and Answers

Benediction... *(prayer coordinator)*

Refreshments and Fellowship

PASTOR'S PRAYER PARTNERS

(Meeting Reminder Postcard or E-mail)
(date)

Friendly Reminder (from pastor _____)

This is just a friendly reminder concerning the organizational
meeting of the Pastor's Prayer Partners that will take place
this Sunday afternoon (date)
at (time)
in (location).

I will be introducing the Pastor's Prayer Partners ministry. I
am excited about this group and what I believe God is going
to do through our prayer ministry.
I look forward to seeing you there.

No Response Letter

(date)

(name & address)

Dear (name):

A few days ago I wrote you concerning a burden I have had on my heart for some time—the beginning of a Pastor's Prayer Partners ministry. I invited you to consider being a part of this initial endeavor with a one-year commitment.

The commitment would involve (1) prayer in the conference room and/or pastor's office one morning service per month; (2) a breakfast meeting with other prayer partners four times a year; (3) a commitment to pray for the pastoral staff and ministry of this church on a consistent basis; and (4) an openness to a focused, personal prayer ministry in your life.

To this point I have not received a response from you. I am not trying to rush an answer, but, I would like to encourage you to respond as soon as possible so we can make necessary arrangements. With this in mind, I am sending you another form for your convenience.

Thank you for your prayerful consideration. I shall be looking forward to hearing from you soon.

God bless you!

Yours in Christ,

(name of pastor)
Enclosure

Negative Reply Letter

(date)

(name & address)

Dear   (name):

Thank you for responding to my request to be a part of the new Pastor's Prayer Partners ministry and for giving it prayerful consideration. I certainly understand your not being able to participate at this time.

While prayer is something in which all of us want to be involved, there are some programs that do not fit into our present schedules. However, please remember us in prayer that God will make this a meaningful and powerful ministry for the enhancement of His work at (name of church).

May God's richest blessings rest upon you!

Yours in Christ,

(pastor)

Pastor's Prayer Partners
BREAKFAST MEETING
(date)

Welcome ....(pastor)

Invocation...(selected prayer partner)

BREAKFAST

Sharing and Q & A ....(pastor)

Choruses ....(selected prayer partner)

Teaching on Process of Prayer .... (pastor, or person designated by pastor)

Prayer Time

    Prayer Requests ....(prayer coordinator)

    Prayer Focus...(pastor)

Matters to Mention

        (Place any announcements here.)

Benediction ....(selected prayer partner)

Full-Day Retreat Schedule
PASTOR'S PRAYER PARTNERS RETREAT
(Place)
(Date)

8:00 a.m.   **Registration & Fellowship**..*donuts and coffee*

8:30 a.m.   **Welcome**...*prayer coordinator*

                Announcements .... *pastor*

                Devotion.. *selected prayer partner*

                Praise and Worship.. *selected prayer partner*

9:00 a.m.   ***Praying for Yourself**...................................... *selected prayer partner*

9:45 a.m.   ***Praying for Your Family**................................ *selected prayer partner*

10:30 a.m.   **Break**

10:45 a.m.   **Praise, Worship & Testimonies**.....................................*prayer coordinator*

11:00 a.m.   ***Praying for Your Leader**... *pastor*

11:45 a.m.   **Lunch**

12:30 p.m.   **Praise & Worship** .... *selected prayer partner*

12:45 p.m.   ***Praying for the Church** .... *selected prayer partner*

1:30 p.m.   **Break**

1:45 p.m.   **Testimonies**

2:00 p.m.   ***Praying for Others**... *selected prayer partner*

2:45 p.m.   **Wrap-up** .... *pastor*

3:00 p.m.   **Benediction** ....*prayer coordinator*

*Allow 20-30 minutes for teaching & 15-25 minutes for prayer time.

Half-Day Retreat Schedule
PASTOR'S PRAYER PARTNERS RETREAT
(Place)   (Date)

8:00 a.m.   **Registration & Fellowship**...*donuts and coffee*

8:30 a.m.   **Welcome & Overview of the Day**... *pastor*
              Sharing ....*prayer coordinator*

              Praise and Worship.. *selected prayer partner*

              Devotion.. *selected prayer partner*

9:00 a.m.   ***Praying for Yourself & Family**.. *selected prayer partner*

9:45 a.m.   ***Praying for Your Church**... *selected prayer partner*

10:20 a.m.   **Break**

10:30 a.m.   **Praise, Worship & Testimonies**... *selected prayer partner*

10:45 a.m.   ***Praying for Others**.. *pastor*

11:20 a.m.   **Lunch**

12:00 p.m.   **Praise & Worship** .... *selected prayer partner*

12:10 p.m.   ***Praying for Your Leader**... *selected prayer partner*

12:45 p.m.   **Wrap-up & Challenge**.. *pastor*

1:00 p.m.   **Benediction**.. *selected prayer partner*

*Allow 20-30 minutes for teaching & 15-25 minutes for prayer time.

The Basics of Prayer

And it came about while He was praying in a certain place, after He had finished; one of His disciples said to Him, Lord, teach us to pray just as John also taught his disciples (Luke 11:1).

Note: This is the only thing the disciples ever asked Jesus to teach them.

Text: Matthew 6:5-15

I. The Person of Prayer (vv.5-8)

Do not be like the . . . (v.5)

Why?

Do not be like the . . . (v.7)

But do . . . (vv.14, 15)

Because?

II. The Procedure of Prayer (v.6)

The Period

The Place

The Privacy

God's greatest men spend time alone with Him (Mark 1:35; 6:46, 47).

The Person

In verses 6-9 this word appears six times.

The Promise

III. The Problem of Prayer (vv. 5, 7)

What is the problem in verse 5?

Why is this a problem?

What is the problem in verse 7?

Why is this a problem?

IV. The Pattern of Prayer (vv. 9-13)

The Process of Prayer

The effectual fervent prayer of a righteous man availeth much (James 5:16).

I. Making Prayer a Habit

A. Problems
1. Finding time
2. Becoming mechanical
3. Purposeless wandering

B. Questions to resolve before a habit of prayer can be found
1. Are you committed to breaking any old patterns that hinder, and forming new ones?
2. Are you in control of your life to make the changes necessary?
3. Are you open to different times and ways to pray?
4. Are you willing to make necessary changes?

II. The Habit of Prayer

A. Steps in initiating a habit of prayer
1. Recognizing the need
2. Making the decision
3. Reinforcing the decision
4. Renewing the perception of prayer
5. Changing the self-perception

B. Results of a habit of prayer

Making Prayer a Personal Delight

Scriptural Lesson: Matthew 21:12-16

Prayer is making an incredible impact on our world. Because of prayer mobilization, strongholds are coming down, barriers are being removed and breakthroughs are forthcoming. This is true across the spectrum from individual lives . . . to churches . . . to united efforts (like community prayer campaigns). For prayer to have its proper place in our lives it needs to become a delight. Let us examine a scriptural example of how this comes about.

I. Jesus made the temple a house of **purity.**

        (by casting out the money changers)

II. Jesus made the house of **purity** into a house of **prayer.**

    A. Prayer first becomes a **desire**.
    B. Prayer next becomes a **discipline**.
    C. Prayer finally becomes a **delight**.

III. Jesus made the house of **prayer** into a house of **power.**

V. Jesus made the house of **power** into a house of **praise.**

Feedback Form

What is the personal vision you feel the Lord has given you for the Pastor's Prayer Partners ministry?

_____

_____

_____

How can we make this ministry more effective?

_____

_____

_____

What can we do to make your daily prayer time more productive?

_____

_____

_____

What kind of helps would enhance the Sunday prayer time in the pastor's office?

_____

_____

_____

How can we make breakfast meetings more desirable and effective?

_____

_____

_____

What would you like to see happen during our retreat?

What suggestions would you have for bringing this about?

_____

_____

_____

Name of Church

website

e-mail

phone

PASTOR'S PRAYER PARTNERS LIST

(Place names and contact info for each member.)

1.   name
     position
     contact info
2.   name
     position
     contact info
3.   etc.

SECTION 10

Resurrection Breakfast
Introduction

Why a Resurrection Breakfast?

Would you like to . . .
- Help men build relationships with unsaved friends?
- Add new life to your men's program?
- Involve men in evangelism?
- Get local churches active in ministry?
- See scores of unchurched men make a first-time commitment to Christ?

Your Answer: The Resurrection Breakfast!

The **Resurrection Breakfast** is an annual soulwinning event held in cities across America on the Saturday morning before Easter Sunday. This event is designed to challenge Christian men from all Evangelical denominations to form a citywide effort to invite other unsaved men to attend a breakfast and to hear a special speaker with a powerful testimony.

Easter is a season that presents a unique opportunity to reach men for Christ. Hearts are normally more tender and open at this time. If properly organized, the **Resurrection Breakfast** will involve your men in an unprecedented outreach to the community. Through this method you will reach men that heretofore would not respond to a church function.

Hundreds of breakfasts have been sponsored in cities across America, Canada, the Bahamas and in other countries. The speakers have included local civic, business, and sports figures; Christian judges, governors, and other elected officials; Christian movie and TV personalities; coaches; or anyone else who might have the name recognition to draw a crowd and present a soulwinning testimony. The results have been fantastic—thousands of men have received Christ as their personal Savior.

We have seen firsthand what God has done through these **Resurrection Breakfasts.** Church growth has occurred during the follow-up phase of these meetings. When men accept Christ at the breakfast, cards are filled out and distributed to area pastors who can then contact the new Christians to bring them into the church and disciple them.

Our vision is to see these soul winning events held simultaneously in many major cities across our country and in small communities through a local men's discipleship chapter. In the larger cities we are asking that the various men's groups from different churches and denominations come together to jointly sponsor what can become a much larger citywide event.

The evangelistic and church growth potential is staggering. If 100 cities would host a Resurrection Breakfast in one year, with a good attendance at each, there could be the potential to see many men come to Christ in one morning! *Please join with us in prayer that this will be a reality.*

Two Things You Need to Do

• Read Through These Guidelines in One Sitting.

The planning and promotion of the **Resurrection Breakfast** is very simple, but it will require you to conceptualize all ideas and details in your mind before you begin making preparations. Look carefully through each of the major areas in this planning guide so you can better understand the *concept* and *action steps*. Please pay particular attention to the section regarding *materials available for free download.* We have carefully considered the entire planning and promotion process. This guide brings to you the fruit of that labor.

• Contact Us!

Men's Discipleship International is ready to help you with any guidance and direction that you may need. We will be happy to share our knowledge and expertise with you. How you begin the planning is an indication of how successful the event will be. Let's do it right! If you have any questions, or need any assistance in planning, please contact us.

Men's Discipleship International
Resurrection Breakfast Event Coordinator
P.O. Box 2430
Cleveland, TN 37320-2430; Phone: 423-478-7286; Fax: 423-478-7288; E-mail:
mensdiscipleship@churchofgod.org; Web site: www.coglifebuilders.com

Concept

The main idea of the Resurrection Breakfast is to challenge Christian men to invite an unsaved male friend to a Saturday morning breakfast prior to Easter Sunday.

We have three goals in mind. **First**, this is to be a soulwinning event with the intent of reaching men for Christ. **Second**, we want to help Christian men accept the challenge to be greater men of God and get involved in ministry. **Finally**, we see a need for men to build bridges of friendship with what we call "men on the fringe." These are unsaved, unchurched, or now "dechurched" men.

An added feature of this outreach is the "built-in" follow-up that naturally occurs when a man accepts Christ. Discipleship begins when the friend who brought him to the breakfast then invites him to church.

The concept works well as an interdenominational citywide event or as a state, district, or local church event. **In planning, bear in mind that a man should not have to drive more than 50-60**

miles (100 kilometers) to attend this meeting. If the Resurrection Breakfast is sponsored by a state, regional, or territorial group, several breakfasts may need to be planned so as to include the entire constituency.

Sponsors

The **Resurrection Breakfast** can be sponsored by any group of men—a state or territorial lay board, a district or local church men's group, or any group of believers who want to get together to reach men for Christ.

Size

The size of this event is not important. We do suggest that, if possible, a goal be set to reach at least 100 men (50 men of the church reaching 50 unsaved). We would consider a large breakfast to be between 300-700 men. It is quite possible that a local church men's group could sponsor an event such as this in a smaller town and it would be acceptable to have fewer men in attendance, half of which would be unchurched. *Note: Avoid at all cost the breakfast becoming only a fellowship of believers.*

Key Ingredients

- **Begin each planning session with prayer** so that all involved can share the burden of winning lost friends and restoring hurting men to Christ.
- **Recruit workers** that are willing to pay the price of diligence and faithfulness.
- **Provide an interesting, anointed speaker** who can effectively relate to the men and convey his personal relationship with the Lord Jesus Christ.
- **Frequently remind** the men of the importance of bringing an unsaved friend, relative, or coworker to the breakfast.
- **Make sure that the speaker,** or a designate, offers an opportunity for men to receive Christ as their personal Savior.
- **Provide a place to pray** with men who wish to make this commitment.
- **Assist in the immediate follow-up** of the new converts (preferably by those who bring them). A commitment card and other excellent materials are available for free download at www.coglifebuilders.com.

Interdenominational

The goal of this meeting is to reach as many men as possible with the good news of Jesus Christ. In order to do this, men from all Evangelical denominations should be involved in inviting unsaved (unchurched) friends. Any born-again believer should be afforded the opportunity to participate in inviting a friend to the breakfast.

Use of Our Logos and Artwork

The name "Resurrection Breakfast" and all logos and artwork are the property of Men's Discipleship International. Anyone receiving this planning guide from us has our permission to use the logos and artwork to plan and sponsor a breakfast. These items are available for viewing and download on our website, www.coglifebuilders.com.

Action Steps

Form a Steering Committee

Begin with men you can count on to be there when you need them and who will get the job done.

The First Meeting

As leader, share your burden for unsaved men in the community. It would be a good idea to begin with group prayer. Ask the men to focus on someone they know who is not a believer and allow plenty of time to pray.

Explain the concept as presented in this planning guide before asking for volunteers and making assignments.

Assign areas of responsibility. Just one person, or a group of men, depending on the size of the breakfast, can do these jobs. The various duties are explained throughout the remainder of this guide.

- Finance
- Promotion
- Facilities (location)
- Program (music and worship)
- Speaker selection
- Ushers and greeters
- Printing

This core group should consist of at least 8-10 men. Any group of committed Christian men can participate such as church council, elders, prayer group, or any lay leaders. Some of the other members could be:

- A member of a local Gideon's Camp.
- Christian Businessmen's Committee.
- Fellowship of Christian Athletes.
- Or any group such as these.

Form the steering committee well in advance of the **Resurrection Breakfast** in order to allow the other committees time to function properly.

Location of Meetings

The best place for the steering committee to meet is where the actual **Resurrection Breakfast** will take place. This will allow all committee members to familiarize themselves with the surroundings and to be comfortable with the physical arrangements.

Frequency

It is suggested that the steering committee meet several times during the planning and promotion of this event. Many details simply cannot be ironed out in only one or two meetings.

Other Needs

- Assign someone to take notes at all of the meetings, i.e., prepare minutes and be responsible to mail them to all members of the steering committee. This person should also establish a committee mailing list with addresses, phone and fax numbers and email contacts.
- Ask someone to be responsible to contact committee members to remind them of the time and place for each meeting.
- Establish a method of financial accountability for the handling of all funds related to the breakfast.
- Make sure an agenda is prepared for each meeting, so the time of busy men will not be wasted deciding what to discuss.

Select and Confirm the Meeting Place

In order to reach the "fringe" men that we have been talking about, it is best not to schedule the **Resurrection Breakfast** at a local church. Most unchurched men are reluctant to visit our "sacred acre."

Since many hotels and meeting rooms are booked many months in advance, you should immediately look for a hotel, or other meeting place with the following qualifications:

- Acceptable quality—Look for superior service and quality meeting rooms.
- Accessibility—The venue should be easily accessible to all attending. For example, it should be centrally located.
- Reasonably priced—The cost of the breakfast should be affordable. Attempt to offer a complete and tasty meal while at the same time covering all expenses. For example, if the meal cost is $7.50 per man, perhaps the ticket charge should be $10.00.
- Be cautious about contracts! Many hotels commit the sponsoring group to pay for an agreed number regardless of the actual attendance. Work very closely with the meeting facility to assure that everything is confirmed prior to any promotional printing. **Identify**

a competent contact person at the meeting facility and get to know him or her personally, but be prepared for personnel changes that can occur frequently.

Select and Confirm the Speaker

The planning process has now reached a critical stage. The selection of the speaker is vital to the success of this meeting. It is permissible to use a layman or clergyman. The ideal speaker is a layman, such as a sports figure with some recognition who will be a "drawing card" for all men, including unsaved men. It is best to use a person who will share his personal testimony briefly (20-30 minutes).

The idea is not to have a "preachimony" or a heavy preaching service. Look for someone who, as part of their presentation, can share the steps one has to take in order to be born again. The leadership should really make this a matter of prayer, and the whole group should agree upon the final choice. The acceptability of the speaker by the men in attendance will determine whether or not the breakfast is successful.

All the terms of the speaker's invitation should be in writing. Verbal contact should first be made with the speaker, followed by a letter. Details concerning the honorarium, travel, food and lodging should be agreed to and understood by everyone up front.

Prepare a Budget

A sample budget form is included in this planning guide. It may be necessary to add or delete certain items based on specific local needs.

Print Advertising Materials

The following items need to be printed and available for free download.

- Four-color posters
- Tickets

Advertise the Breakfast

- Mail the promotional letter (see sample letter in this section).
- Put posters in strategic locations.
- Promote in area churches and other denominations.
- Promote among business and professional people.

Additional Ideas

Design a schedule of promotion for Christian business and professional people. Plan a strategy for distributing a promotional brochure/poster and other advertising to your mailing list. Be sure to include a way for them to contact you to commit and confirm ticket purchases, etc. Use the media to help promote the meeting! Design a schedule for promotion including newspaper advertisements, television and radio coverage, denominational periodicals and newsletters, mailings to constituents of involved churches, as well as a mailing to area pastors.

Promote the Event

Now that the steering committee is formed, the budget has been prepared, the speakers and workers selected, and all of the printed materials are ready, we begin the important stage of promotion. Here are the steps involved:

Schedule personal visits to churches, local men's groups, Full Gospel Businessmen's Fellowships, or anywhere Christian men are meeting. At this time, distribute posters, explain the meeting concept, and give challenges to the churches or groups to buy tables.

- **Use the concept of tickets "sold as tables." Very important**—it is best to sell tickets according to the number of seats per table (up to 10 each). For example, a church is challenged to buy three tables, which will hold 30 men, and then the church will challenge 15 of its male members to bring 15 unsaved men to the meeting. This is a very crucial point since it helps build momentum, and it is difficult to fill a huge room if you sell individual tickets at first. Additionally, many businesses or individuals may wish to sponsor one or more tables.
- **Send letters advertising the meeting**. (See sample letter.)
- **Use poster.**
- **Make phone calls**. Call everybody! Get the word out; make sure people know that the **Resurrection Breakfast** is happening in their community.
- **Make personal contacts**. It is recommended that you contact everyone you know to announce this meeting. Call influential businessmen in the community who will encourage men to attend this meeting.
- **Send sign-up sheets to the churches**. In one of the mailings to the churches, send a printed sign-up sheet for placing on the bulletin board or table in the church foyer. This will remind men to sign up early to secure their places at the breakfast.

Activate Program Committee

Select Song Leader, Moderator, Musicians

Careful consideration should be given to the selection of the song leader since he is the first person on the program. The man selected should be experienced in making men comfortable and encouraging them to sing, especially those who are not frequently in church.

The musicians should be capable of handling any task they are asked to do in the music area. Once selected, they should be informed of the committee's expectations. As with the speaker, if there are honorariums for the song leader and/or the musicians, these should be agreed to and understood by everyone up front.

The moderator should have a sense of humor and be a good communicator. However, he should not be a "wordy" person, but rather, capable of keeping the meeting flowing.

Prepare the Program

Here is a sample Order of Service:

- Welcome/Greeting/Opening Prayer
- Meal
- Choruses
- Special Songs (1 or 2)
- Introductions
- Speaker
- Commitment
- Closing (sign commitment card, receive offering, mention Bibles, books, and tracts for the men if you decide to make these available)

Prepare the Hotel Room for the Breakfast

- **Print a banner** (if possible). It should be 20-30 feet (7-10 meters) long to be placed behind the head table with the **Resurrection Breakfast** logo and a big **"W E L C O M E."**
- **Secure an adequate sound system**. Many hotels and other meeting rooms have inadequate sound systems. Perhaps a local church will provide a sound system to assure proper amplification. Be sure to check on this important item.
- **Arrange the head table**. Prepare place cards for each person and place them on the table well in advance. The head table should seat no more than 12 people.
- **Request the meeting facility to number the tables**. In this manner groups of men can be directed to their table with ease.
- **Save a table close to the front for the musicians and other special invited guests.**
- **At the close of the meeting, collect all offering (gift) envelopes and commitment cards.**

Other notes

- Pick up the speaker at the airport.
- Secure a hotel room for the speaker.
- Receive an offering and give the men the opportunity to share a gift of money. This money can be set aside to help sponsor a breakfast the following year. It is acceptable to receive an offering for the speaker in a tactful way following his message.
- Forward movement. Because there will be many unchurched men at the **Resurrection Breakfast**, there should be *no* "forward movement." It is best that each man pray at his table. Remember that a Christian invites each one and the one-on-one commitment would be most practical at this point.

Assign Ushers and Greeters

Ushers and greeters should be selected to assist during the actual event. They should help sell and/or collect tickets at the door, assist with seating, distribute programs and other literature, and help with commitment cards, obtain names and addresses, etc. Greeters should help to welcome special guests, seat them in the designated areas, and make all participants feel at ease. Also, both the ushers and greeters can assist with the offering.

Resources

Materials available for free download:

- Event Program
- Logos
- Tickets
- Poster
- Commitment Card
- This Planning Guide Section
- Report Form
- 1 On 1 Invitation Card, http://trinityonlinesolutions.com/contact-info (Note - There is cost for personalization.)

Sample Promotional Letter

(**Resurrection Breakfast** Logo)

(Date)

(City, State, Zip)

Dear Pastor or Men's Leader [personalize if possible]:

We are very excited about a special meeting coming to [**your city**]. It is the ***Resurrection Breakfast*** scheduled for Saturday morning, [**date**]. Please accept our cordial invitation to attend this men's event with us. I am sure that you face the same dilemma as many leaders do—the challenge of getting men involved in helping others to know about Jesus Christ. We are offering you a prime opportunity to be involved in a soulwinning event that will activate laymen, as well as help lost men to hear about the Savior.

The concept is simple: It is a breakfast on the Saturday morning before Easter. It is for all men, and it is time for Christian men to invite their unsaved loved ones, friends, and business associates to come to a meeting where the gospel will be presented. Our keynote speaker is [name of speaker]. We know that he is a man who has a dynamic testimony of the saving grace of Jesus Christ. This will be a time of celebration and commitment for men as we worship together.

We are counting on you. Will you help us? Will you place one of the enclosed posters on your bulletin board and give the other one to a leading layman in your congregation? If possible, we would like for you to challenge each man in your church to buy a ticket for himself and for an unsaved friend. We are selling tickets by tables. We would like for you to buy at least one table at the cost of [price] per ticket—which would be $[total price] per table. This will be a time for you to encourage your men to become real soulwinners.

Please pray about this and order your tickets soon.

In His service,

[name] Steering Committee

Enclosures—Poster, Sign-Up Form

Sample Budget

(Be sure to add the projected costs of any new items you have created locally that are not part of the original packet).

1. Steering Committee Meeting Expense $_____

2. Decorations/Set-up (if necessary) $_____

3. Audio Taping $_____

4. Literature $_____

      a.   Poster $_____

      b.   Tickets $_____

      c.   Letterhead $_____

      d.   Envelopes $_____

      e.   Banner $_____

5. Speaker/Honorarium $_____

6. Special Music/Musicians (could be donated) $_____

7. Breakfast Meal $_____

8. Gratis Meals (for speaker and special guests) $_____

9. Postage and Telephone $_____

10. Event Program $_____

11. Name Badges/Soulwinning Tract/Gift Envelope $_____

12. Other $_____

             Total $_____

Sign-up Form

"Sharing the Life of the Living Lord With Others"

Eastertime is a historic opportunity for men to reach out and share the life of our Lord with other men.

Help us by participating in the following three resurrection outreach activities.

- The Spirit of Life —— Praying for others

- The Voice of Life —— Making telephone calls

- The Journey of Life —— Bringing others to the breakfast

"I am the resurrection and the life …" (John 11:25). "In Him was life, and the life was the light of men" (John 1:4). "I have come that they may have life, and that they may have it more abundantly" (John 10:10).

I will be a part of the Resurrection Breakfast

Name _____

Address _____

City/State/Zip _____

Please return this form to _____

SECTION 11

Get Connected

Church of God Men's Discipleship
David H. Gosnell, International Coordinator
P O Box 2430
2490 Keith Street NW
Cleveland, TN 37320

www.coglifebuilders.com
mensdiscipleship@churchofgod.org
888-766-9009 ◆ 423-478-7286

An updated list of each state/regional men's leaders
can be found on our website above.

SECTION 12

Discipleship, Its Program, Process, Priority & Productivity

by Mike Wells

ISBN: 978-1-59684-719-4

This book is dedicated to my mother Shirley Wells, who first introduced me to the Christian faith, to my wife Lisa, who has supported me without hesitancy over the last twenty-five years in my ministry endeavors, and to my daughter Kristin, who has blossomed into a beautiful Christian young lady.

A Word From the Author

What is the mission of the Christian church? This question has been and continues to be on the minds of Christians everywhere, ranging from the time of Jesus' day even into the 21st century. Various answers have been given. First, some believe the church's primary mission is to be a preserver of biblical truth and *"to continue in the apostles' doctrine"* in light of the spiritual deception that exists in the world today (1 Timothy 4:1; Acts 2:42). Second, there are many who believe that the foremost mission of the church is to provide for the physical and material needs of humankind. The Scriptures are clear that the church is to feed the hungry, minister to the sick, clothe the needy, as well as visit those that are incarcerated (Matthew 25:35-40). Additionally, the Bible directs us *to visit orphans and widows in their trouble* (James 1:27). Further, the apostle John exhorts, *But whoever has this world's goods, and sees his brother in need, and shuts up his heart from him, how does the love of God abide in him?* (1 John 3:17).

While there is merit to both of these opinions regarding the church's mission, the best way to truly answer this question is to recall the words of Jesus as recorded in Matthew 28:19-20 where it says, **Go therefore and make disciples of all the nations, baptizing them in the name of the Father and of the Son and of the Holy Spirit . . . Teaching them to observe all things I have commanded you. . . .** Jesus points out that the overall mission of the Christian church is twofold: 1) evangelize the sinner; and 2) disciple the believer. This being said, it has been my personal observation over the years that the church has done exceptionally well with world evangelization, but not so well in its efforts to make disciples. That being the case, this book was written to provide a basic understanding of what being a disciple of Christ is, as well as how to grow in our discipleship with Christ. In the book we will examine the program for making disciples, the process of becoming a disciple, the priority of being a disciple, and finally, the productivity of a disciple. It is my sincere prayer that as you work through this foundational study, you will find the material helpful and instructional, as well as that you may "grow in the grace and knowledge of our Lord and Savior Jesus Christ" (2 Peter 3:18).

–Michael L. Wells

Table of Contents

FOREWORD

Mike Wells is my close and personal friend for many, many years now. He has served with me in Ministerial Development since 1993 and throughout our lives, we have shared journey as fellow pastors, peers, pupils, and professors. Consequently, I can say, I know him well. Here is what I know . . . Mike is a scholar, a theologian, and a pulpiteer whose convictions about the integrity of the Word are profound. Yet, he is a pastor with a parish he dearly loves, people he serves daily in the toil and grind of dutiful ministry, striving conscientiously to lead each believer to fully mature discipleship in Jesus Christ. That he is so talented in his capacities to study and communicate the truth of the Word, he is yet so down-to-earth practical, having learned how to make truth bite-size, digestible, easy to consume and nourish the spirit and soul.

I cannot patronize a dearest friend; I must say what I believe to be true: this new discipleship study guide, *Discipleship: Its Program, Process, Priority, and Productivity,* is the absolutely best-written tool for personal spiritual growth I have ever read! The author has so thoroughly covered every important aspect of biblical discipleship possible in this fairly concise manual, and yet, has not made it ivory-tower elusive nor theologically-complex that even the youngest of youth, nor the newest of converts could not understand it. Mike Wells has made this study almost narrative in its presentation, succinctly following a well-defined path of study along the route of discipleship, making *program, process, priority, and productivity* interesting, landmark stops along the way.

Overflowing with Scripture and explanatory insights, the author has consulted the original language *without* making the study intimidating or busy. There are just enough academics in the study to make it scholarly and credible, yet plenty enough practical application to make it personal and pragmatic! The insights for each of the discipleship lessons presented are so rich with truth, yet so lush with intrigue, that the reader will be tempted to "race to the end' rather than "stop and ponder" the meaningful tips surely to change his life with simple application. Further, the author has strategically placed very invoking reflections and questions throughout this manual that challenge the reader to *participate* in the lessons, writing out his own thoughts to "test" his comprehension of the material.

This manual, *will become the standard* for discipleship development in the Church of God; perhaps the ideal. It is a practical tool that can be used in small groups, new convert classes, sermon series, corporate Bible study, or simply as a personal self-study for the ambitious, conscientious student of the Word. It can aptly be used as a course unit in Bible college curriculum and not fall short its accreditation quality. The Church of God Men's Discipleship coordinator, Bishop David Gosnell, is to be commended for having recruited this author to prepare this manual. It will be an invaluable resource for stimulating and motivating discipleship training in Church of God congregations all over the world.

Enjoy the journey! It truly leads somewhere worth going!

–Pastor Wayne Flora, M.Div., D.Min
MIP Coordinator, ENC

Introduction

Oftentimes as a person is entering his or her final days on earth they will speak words that are foremost on their mind, as well as the things that are most important to them. This certainly was the case with Jesus shortly after His resurrection and just a few days prior to His ascension. Some of the last words He spoke are recorded in Matthew 28:19-20 which state:

> *Go therefore and make disciples of all nations, baptizing them in the name of the Father and of the Son and of the Holy Spirit. Teaching them to observe all things that I have commanded you; and lo, I am with you always, even to the end of the age.*

Clearly these words are a missional mandate given by Christ to His followers in the first-century church, but they are applicable to the 21st century church as well. In a concise manner of speaking Jesus says the mission of the church is to disciple the people of God so that they can affect the world for Christ. If it is the mandate of Christ for the church to ***make disciples***, then His will for individual believers is that we ***become disciples***. Raymond Culpepper, presiding bishop of the Church of God, issued a challenge to the denomination at the 2010 General Assembly to ***Engage the Missional Mandate*** as outlined by Jesus in his "last" but "lasting words" of Matthew 28:19-20. Taking this challenge seriously the offices of Men's and Women's Discipleship have embarked upon a journey to assist Church of God people nationwide. This journey would afford them the opportunity to ***become disciples*** of Christ and better prepare them to ***make disciples*** for Christ. The book you now are reading is a product of this effort and throughout the next four weeks the topic of discipleship will be covered and in so doing we will learn what it means to be a disciple of Christ, as well as examine such topics as the program for making disciples, the process of becoming a disciple, the price and priority of being a disciple, and finally, the profile and productivity of a disciple. It is my sincere prayer that you will not only become a more deeply committed disciple of Christ through this study, but that also you will become a more effective maker of disciples for Christ.

The Program of Making Disciples

Bill Hull in his book *The Disciple-Making Pastor* points out that "disciple-making takes more faith than any other task of the church." Nevertheless, it should become the heartbeat of the church because it is the heartbeat of God. The program that God has given to the church to make disciples is called The Great Commission. Raymond Culpepper, in his book *The Great Commission: The Solution* says, "*The* because there is one premier mission of the church. *Great* because the mission is preeminent. *Commission* because it is the assigned marching orders of the Spirit-filled church." It is further stated that Jesus died for the mission, and we (the church) live to finish or complete the mission. Therefore, when we come down to the end of our earthly journey like Jesus we can say, "It is finished," and "I (we-the church) have finished the work You have given me (us) to do" (John 19:30; 17:4). Matthew records The Great Commission in the aforementioned reference (Matthew 28:19-20), however, it is mentioned as well by the three other Gospel writers.

In Mark's reference of the Great Commission, Jesus says that we are to preach the gospel to whom? Read Mark 16:15 and write the answer in the line below.

_____

In Luke's version of the Great Commission, what was/is to be the nature or content of the message in carrying out the mission of the church? Read Luke 24:46-47 and write the answer on the line provided.

_____

Read John 20:21 and write on the line below what Jesus meant when he said, "As the Father has sent Me, I also send you."

_____

Before issuing the Great Commission, Jesus established the foundation upon which the success of the disciples' ministry, as well as that of the 21st century is dependent upon. He said, "**All authority (power) has been given to Me in heaven and on the earth**" (v.18). The word *authority* (power) here refers to delegated power along with the right to use it. Furthermore, it implies "all the right of absolute authority and all the resources of absolute power." That is, the word carries the idea of an active power that transcends all physical, political, and spiritual realms. Thus when we begin to fulfill the Great Commission of making disciples we do not go forth in the power of just anyone, but rather with and in the full authority of Jesus Christ, King of Kings and Lord of Lords. Without this ultimate authority backing them in the disciple-making mission, the followers of Jesus would have been fruitless in their labors and the same truth applies to the 21st-century church as well.

Prior to His ascension Jesus issued what command to His disciples in Luke 24:49? Explain briefly in your own words on the lines below the significance of this command as it relates to fulfilling of the Great Commission to make disciples.

_____

_____

In Acts 1:8 Jesus says that we will be empowered how/when for Christian service and the mandated mission of making disciples? Explain your answer on the lines below.

_____

_____

With an understanding now of the authority Jesus gives us when participating in the fulfillment of the missional mandate, let's look now at the actual program employed by Jesus' followers, and us to make disciples. The heart of the Great Commission is Matthew 28:19-20. These verses give us the blueprint, the methods, and methodology for fulfilling the command of Christ. Three important elements are given by Jesus as to the program for **making disciples**: *going, baptizing,* and *teaching.* "**Making Disciples**" is in the form of a command while "**baptizing**" and "**teaching**" provide the means by which we make disciples. Often we get the first part of the Commission (world evangelization) and fail to implement the latter part of making disciples. In other words, the church has put forth great effort to evangelize the sinner, but less effort to disciple the believer. Simply put, as Bill Hull has said, "the church has tried to get world evangelization without disciple making," thus he adds, the Great Commission has been "worshipped, but not obeyed."

Fulfilling the Great Commission begins with *going.* This word can be translated "when you have 'gone,' or 'as you are going.'" It does mean traveling but not always crossing geographical borders. The implication of Jesus' mandate is that "wherever" you are to participate in expanding the kingdom of God on earth. In other words, as you are traveling through life, whether it's foreign, or local, the work of making disciples is for every member of the church, both clergy and laity.

In Matthew 5:13-16 Jesus says believers are "the salt of the earth" and "the light of the world." Explain in your own words on the lines below what this means and how you can fulfill this role on earth.

_____

_____

_____

_____

In Acts 1:8, where did Jesus say world evangelization and disciple making was to take place? After answering, from this verse please explain in your own words how this applies to the 21st-century church.

_____

_____

_____

_____

When Jesus says, "*Go*" it means crossing boundaries to make disciples—crossing over the street to your neighbors, going to meet an unbelieving friend for dinner, going into the inner city (even in places that you may not like, or that are not pleasant), or going out of your comfort zone to share the gospel for the purpose of making disciples. Jesus in His ministry certainly illustrated this point for us. Consider these examples from His life.

- Jesus crossed the boundaries into Samaria to share the news of eternal life with a woman at the well (John 4:1-15).
- Jesus associated with "publicans and sinners" even to the point of going into their houses (Luke 15:1-2).

Read the Book of Jonah and see how God commissioned him to go into Nineveh and watch his reaction. Has God ever asked you to share the gospel with someone that maybe you didn't particularly like, or go to a place that was not so pleasant? If so, did you respond in the same way as Jonah? Write how you reacted on the lines below.

_____

_____

_____

The mission of disciple making is not only for clergy but laity as well. Read Acts 8:26-39 and note how God used a layperson (Philip) to make a disciple of the Ethiopian man. What method did Philip use to make a disciple of this man? Write your answer on the line below.

_____

_____

_____

In 2 Corinthians 5:14 Paul said it was "the love of Christ" that compelled him to make disciples. Explain in your own words on the lines below what the phrase "love of Christ" means. Does it mean Christ's love for him, his love for Christ, or Christ's love for the world? What motivates you to fulfill the Great Commission mandate to make disciples?

_____

_____

_____

_____

The thrust of Jesus' words in Matthew 28:19 is to "*make disciples*." He did not say, "make converts," or "make Christians." What does it mean to make disciples? This involves the reproduction in others of what Christ has produced in us: faith, obedience, growth, authority, compassion, love, and a bold, truthful message as His witnesses or ambassadors. Tony Evans, in his book *What Matters Most* defines discipleship (disciple making) in this manner: " Discipleship (disciple making) is that developmental process of the local church that progressively brings Christians from spiritual infancy to spiritual maturity so they are then able to reproduce the process with someone else." In other words, disciples are to turn around and make other disciples. Paul charged Timothy in 2 Timothy 2:1-2 to reproduce in others what had been produced in him. It states:

> *You therefore, my son, be strong in the grace that is in Christ Jesus. And the things that you have heard from me among many witnesses, commit these to faithful men who will be able to teach others also.*

Paul is challenging Timothy to do with the next generation of people what Paul did with him: pass on the truth of Christ. In other words, it is a transferable process. So to make disciples we are to teach someone else what God has worked into our lives.

Timothy would be able to pass on the truth of Christ to the next generation only if he followed what Paul admonished him to do in 2 Timothy 3:14-15. What did the apostle admonish Timothy to do in verse 14? Write your answer on the line below.

Why, according to Hebrews 5:12, were the Christians not able to teach others? Why were they not able to make disciples? Write your answer on the line below.

Two more means by which we make disciples is *"baptizing"* and *"teaching."* The former is closely associated with the decision of faith (Acts 2:38; 8:36-38) and could rightly represent here a way of summarizing the evangelistic effort of our mission. It marks a person's entrance into the community of faith (Romans 6:1-4). The latter could be summarized as the other half of our mission—the edification or building up of those who are believers. That is, we are to take believers at every stage of spiritual maturity to the next stage of growth (Ephesians 4:11-16). According to Jesus we are not only to teach content (doctrine), but also how to live a life of obedience. This is indicated by His words, "**teaching them to observe all things that I have commanded you . . .**"

If the mission of the church is to make disciples who then are we to disciple? Jesus says, "**of all the nations . . .**" This phrase can also be translated "all the peoples." It derives from the term *ethnos*, meaning "peoples, ethnic groups." Jesus uses the same word in Matthew 24:14 where he says, "And this gospel of the kingdom will be preached in all the world as a witness to the nations, and then the end shall come." Here Jesus says that the universal proclamation of the gospel and fulfillment of the Great Commission would lead to His coming. It is interesting to note that Matthew which was written for the Jewish community would conclude with a reference to the nations. It is almost as though Jesus was addressing their prejudices and challenging them to unify in order to fulfill the Great Commission. In other words, Jesus wants disciples to be made among all the different groups. Revelation 7:9 presents a beautiful portrait of heaven with all the ethnic groups who have been made disciples through the fulfillment of the Great Commission. It declares:

> *After these things I looked, and behold, a great multitude which no one could number, of all the nations, tribes, peoples, tongues, standing before the throne and before the Lamb, clothed with white robes, with palm branches in their hands.*

The Gospel according to Paul is to be preached first to whom in Romans 1:16 and then to whom? Write your answer on the line below.

_____

In 1 Timothy 2:4 Paul says it is the will of God for who is to be saved? Write your answer on the line below.

_____

What can you as a follower of Jesus Christ do to ensure that disciples are made of all nations? Write your answer on the line below.

_____

God's universal love is illustrated by Jesus in His conversation with the religious leader Nicodemus. Take a fresh look at John 3:16 and state in your own words what Jesus meant by the term *world*. Write your answer on the line below.

_____

Jesus concludes His teaching on the Great Commission with a promise that says, "**I am with you always** . . . " and could read, "I myself am continually with you always until the end of the age." In other words, He will be with us every step of the way. Jesus' words remind us of some other great promises given to Moses (Exodus 3:12) and Joshua (Joshua 1:5). Read these verses and write on the line below what God promised these two leaders in the Old Testament.

In closing, the Great Commission (vv. 19-20) is preceded by a reference to Jesus' universal authority (power) and followed by a promise of Jesus' spiritual presence. Both are necessary if we are to fulfill our God-given mission to make disciples.

The Process of Becoming a Disciple

If the missional mandate for the church is to make disciples, and the will of God for individual believers is to become a disciple, then the question must be posed, "What is the definition of a disciple, and what does a disciple do?" The concept of discipleship predates the New Testament era of history. In fact, it was a well-established concept centuries before the birth of Christ. Discipleship is rooted in the Greek world and was practiced by Plato, who is commonly referred to as "the father of philosophy." It was through this process that he trained his student Aristotle, who in turn formed academies through which he could transfer the knowledge he gained to others. Tony Evans, in his book *What Matters Most* notes that this form of "discipling others" was so highly successful that the Greeks used it to influence the entire Greco-Roman world through a process referred to as "Hellenization," which afforded people who were not Greek to be trained in and learn Greek thinking, language, and culture. During the New Testament days this ancient concept was picked up and implemented in a spiritual context so that we could know what it means to be a disciple of Jesus Christ. With a brief understanding of the concept of discipleship and its history, let's develop more fully the definition of a disciple and the process by which one becomes a disciple of Christ. It is important first to explore the definition of a disciple. *Discipleship* is a commonly heard term within Evangelical churches; however, there are many misconceptions related to the definition of this word. Bill Hull, in his great text titled *The Disciple-Making Pastor,* observes that many simply define it as really "getting serious" about Christ, but because of the erroneous understanding of these words many people resist it. He further states that it is often perceived from a very narrow perspective and viewed only as a "cookie-cutter life of Scripture memorization, half-days in prayer, analytical Bible study, door-to-door evangelism, and the forsaking of life's pleasures." Certainly, Scripture memorization, prayer, personal evangelism and Bible study, among other things, are part of being a disciple of Christ, but the definition is much more involved than what has been stated to this point.

Write on the lines below your personal definition of the terms *discipleship* and *disciple*. At the end of the lesson compare it with the biblical definition we will attempt to establish as we go deeper into this study.

_____

_____

_____

_____

In Matthew's account of the Great Commission (Matthew 28:19-20), the phrase "make disciples" is translated from the verb, *matheteuo* which is a derivative of the word *mathetes*, and appears over 250 times, entirely in the Gospels (Matthew, Mark, Luke and John) and Acts. It carries the basic definition of "disciple, pupil, one who learns from another, and normally indicates a person whose life is bound up with that of Jesus, his Master." Further, the verb form of this word (*matheteuo)* means to become a disciple (Matthew 27:57) or to be instructed (Matthew 13:52). There is a great deal of evidence that this concept of discipleship was existent even in the Jewish culture. This is illustrated by the teaching of various traditions through special feasts (e.g. the Passover), as well as in the Jewish home. Generally the focus of this instruction would be from the Pentateuch (Genesis-Deuteronomy), meaning the five books of Moses. The father especially was directly responsible for communicating to his children the Torah, or the teachings of the Law (Deuteronomy 6:6-9). During the New Testament era the apostle Paul was such an example, as he left home to study under the renowned Jewish rabbi, Gamaliel (Acts 5:34; 22:3).

Write on the lines below ways you personally can become a disciple of Christ as described in the above definitions.

_____

_____

_____

_____

If you are a parent, list on the lines below ways you can communicate these scriptural truths to your children.

_____

_____

_____

_____

Now that we have a basic definition of a disciple, let's turn our attention to how this term is employed in the New Testament. Avery T. Willis, Jr., in his study on discipleship titled *The Disciple's Cross,* identifies three usages of the word *disciple* by the New Testament authors. Study reveals that the word *disciple* is used three ways by the New Testament authors: First, the word *disciple* speaks specifically of a person who is devoted to a particular group or teacher. Mark 2:18 illustrates this usage and declares:

> *The disciples of John and of the Pharisees were fasting. Then they came and said to Him, Why do the disciples of John and of the Pharisees fast, but Your disciples do not fast?*

On the lines below identify the three groups noted by Mark who have disciples.

_____

_____

_____

_____

(b) Second, the term *disciple* denotes the apostles of Jesus who were called by Him.

Mark specifically speaks of the appointing of apostles by Jesus. Mark 3:14 states: *Then He appointed twelve, that they might be with Him and that he might send them out to preach.*

In Mark 3:15 what type of ministry is given to the apostles appointed by Jesus? Write your answer on the lines below.

_____

_____

(c) Third, the word *disciple* describes a follower of Jesus who meets specified requirements. Read Luke 14:26-27 and write on the lines below what requirements a disciple of Jesus is supposed to meet.

_____

_____

_____

_____

Jesus, the supreme disciple maker defined a disciple in various ways throughout his earthly ministry. Bill Hull, in *The Disciple-Making Pastor*, provides the following summary of Jesus' definitions of a disciple. A disciple:

- Is willing to deny self, take up a cross daily, and follow Him (Luke 9:23-25).
- Puts Christ before self, family, and possessions (Luke 14:25-35).
- Is committed to Christ's teachings (John 8:31).
- Is committed to world evangelism (Matthew 9:36-38).
- Love others as Christ loves (John 13:34-35).
- Abides in Christ, is obedient, bears fruit, glorifies God, has joy and loves the brethren (John 15:7-17).

Three separate times Jesus emphatically declares that if any person is not willing to make such commitments, then he "cannot be my disciple" (Luke 14:25, 26, 33).

After reading the definitions of a disciple provided by Jesus, how would you personally assess your life in accordance with them, and how are you striving to fulfill each of the requirements in your life? Write your answers on the lines below.

_____

_____

_____

_____

Becoming a disciple of Jesus Christ is not an event, but a process. The process is not automatic but one that is a lifelong pursuit. It begins with a spiritual birth and is a process that continues as one of spiritual maturation and growth. The spiritual birth that gains us entrance into God's kingdom is described in John 3:1-8 where Jesus is speaking to Nicodemus, a religious leader of that day. Pointedly Jesus says to Nicodemus: "Most assuredly, I say to you, unless one is born again (born from above), he cannot see the kingdom of God . . . Most assuredly, I say to you, unless one is born of water and the Spirit, he cannot enter the kingdom of God" (John 3:3,5). The spiritual rebirth spoken of here comes about when a person places his or her faith and trust in the finished work of Christ on the cross, and receives forgiveness for ones sin.

Why, according to John 3:3, does Jesus say being "born again" is important? Write your answer on the line below.

_____

The moment one receives Christ as Savior in the full pardon of sins a spiritual transfer takes place. Paul describes this transfer in Colossians 1:13-14 which says:

He has delivered us from the power of darkness and conveyed [transferred] us into the kingdom of the Son of His love, in whom we have redemption through His blood, the forgiveness of sins.

Because we have been delivered from the kingdom of darkness and transferred to the Kingdom of light, what does 1 Peter 2:9 say we are to do? Write your answer on the line below.

_____

Jesus in Matthew 11:28-30 describes the process toward discipleship that follows after conversion or regeneration. He declares:

Come to Me, all you labor and are heavy laden, and I will give you rest. Take My yoke upon you and learn from Me, for I am gentle and lowly in heart, and you will find rest for your souls. For My yoke is easy and My burden is light.

The immediate context of this text is the rejection of Jesus as the Messiah by the Jewish people, and the beginning appeal that would be made to the surrounding Gentile nations toward accepting Him as Messiah. Here Jesus declares emphatically that true discipleship can be enjoyed only by those who come to Him in childlike faith. Tony Evans points out that Jesus did not say, "Come to my teaching," or "Come to my miracles," but "**Come to me.**" Some writers interpret this to be a call to salvation. This invitation is extended to "**all who labor and are heavy laden,**" or "to all who are tired from hard toil," and "to all who are loaded down." Various definitions have been given to these phrases and can be summarized by the following four statements: 1) sin, 2) excessive demands of religious leaders, 3) oppression and persecution, or 4) weariness in the search for God, as well as carrying the load of burden which makes one weary. Regardless of what way these phrases are interpreted, the clear-cut call of Jesus is to respond positively to His invitation, first to accept Him as Savior, and second, to become His disciple. He then says, "**I will give you rest**." In other words, "I will rest you," that is, with My presence. After extending an invitation to the tired and burdened down, Jesus says, "**Take My yoke upon you and learn from Me . . .**" This is to be done at the initiative of each person because Jesus will not put it upon us without our consent. In other words, it is a personal choice whether or not we want to become a disciple of Jesus Christ. With this understanding of verse 29, many interpret it to be a call to discipleship. In the day of Jesus, a yoke according to the book *New Manners and Customs of the Bible* was a wooden frame placed on the backs and shoulders of oxen to make them pull in tandem. Simple yokes consisted of a bar with two loops either of rope or wood that went around the animal's neck. More elaborate yokes constructed from shafts were placed on the necks of these animals that enabled them to plow. They were almost like fitted collar-like frames, shaped to rest on the neck and shoulders of two animals teamed together. Now that we have a basic understanding of a literal yoke that was used for multiple purposes during that day, what does Jesus mean by "**My yoke**?" One writer interprets it as the discipline of discipleship, while another views it as the submission of discipleship meaning that as a disciple of Jesus Christ we come under His Lordship. Also, there are some who regard the yoke as representing our companionship with Christ. First, with regard to the discipline of discipleship, one needs to understand that the religious leaders of that day were placing people under tremendous bondage by requiring of them excessive religious obligations that resulted in suppression, that is, more of a works righteousness (Matthew 23: 4; Acts 15:10) rather than a relationship with God through His grace by faith.

What does Paul teach in Ephesians 2:8-9 and Titus 3:5 about our salvation? Does it happen as a result of God's grace or our righteous deeds? Write your answers on the lines provided.

_____

_____

_____

According to Titus 2:12 what does the grace of God teach that we as disciples should do? Write your answer on the lines below.

_____

_____

_____

Rabbinical teaching of that time period spoke of taking on the "yoke of the Law" and under this the burdens of people became oppressively heavy. That is, trying to keep all the outlined requirements created a spiritual heaviness for them. That is why Jesus exhorted the people, "**Take My yoke upon you and learn from Me, for I am gentle and lowly in heart, and you will find rest for your souls.**" Jesus' yoke by way of contrast is **easy** and his **burden is light.** They are not so because His call to discipleship is less demanding but because it makes us pupils of One who is gentle and humble in heart. That is, Jesus is more interested in our relationship with and to Him rather than our religiosity before Him. Further, the purpose of Christian discipleship is to be in submission to Jesus, that is, under His control. Taking the yoke of Jesus also implies that we are harnessed to Him, to work alongside Him. It is a call to Christian service and responsibility. Thus we are to walk with Him because He has a purpose for our life.

In Ephesians 2:8-9 Paul declares that we are saved by grace through faith but for what purpose? Read Ephesians 2:10 and write down your answer on the lines below.

_____

_____

Another implication of taking the yoke of Jesus upon us is that it is His yoke too. Notice He said, "**My yoke**." This means that He is in partnership with us. In ancient times a common practice was to yoke a young ox with an older, more experienced one. First, this was done so that the young more inexperienced ox could learn from the older more experienced one. Did not Jesus say, "**learn of me?**" He is saying, "Come and be discipled by Me." To learn (*mathete*) from Him is to be His disciple (*mathetes*). Matthew 10:25 says: *It is enough for a disciple that he be like his teacher, and a servant like his master . . .*

One definition of disciple means "learner." In his book *What a Way to Live*, Tony Evans has observed that this form of the word *disciple* implies a student who follows the teachings and patterns of his or her teacher so closely that they become almost a "clone" of the teacher. Further, he states that this understanding of the term *disciple* indicates an apprentice that is trained by a skilled master to learn a particular trade. That is, we are to become like Jesus.

In Romans 8:29 Paul states that God's purpose for our life is to be what? Read the verse and write your answer on the line below.

_____

Taking on the yoke of Christ also indicates companionship. In ancient times when the farmer would yoke two oxen together, a younger one with an older one, it would be for the purpose of the latter to bear the brunt of the weight. That is, the older one became the "burden bearer." The same is true with Jesus. When we yoke our lives to Him He becomes our burden bearer. Today, taking on the yoke that links us to Jesus, we too find "**rest**" for our spiritual and emotional person. We walk beside Him, learn from Him, and because our older, stronger, and more powerful companion takes the fullest share of the load our burdens are "**easy and light**."

In the last part of our study we focused on the process of becoming a disciple of Jesus. The process of becoming a disciple includes answering Jesus' invitation to salvation, submission to His lordship, partnering together with Him in ministry, and finally, allowing Him to bear our burdens. But discipleship is also a process of spiritual development. Tony Evans, in *What Matters Most,* points out that our ultimate goal is spiritual maturation; that is, becoming a full-grown, well-developed disciple of Jesus Christ. The context in which this spiritual maturation takes place is the church. In fact, there can be no discipleship outside of the context of the local church. This is true because of the nature of the church as indicated by Paul in 1 Timothy 3:15 which states:

> But if I am delayed, I write so that you may know how you ought to conduct yourself in the house of God which is the church of the living God, the pillar and ground of the truth.

In your own words write what you think Paul means in the previously written verse of 1 Timothy 3:15. Your answer may be written on the lines below.

_____

_____

_____

Additionally, the nurture of the church is important in developing as a disciple of Jesus Christ. The writer of Hebrews speaks of the importance and necessity of assembling together in the local church with fellow believers. Hebrews 10:24-25 expresses the purpose for doing so. It declares:

> _And let us consider one another in order to stir up love and good works, not forsaking the assembling of ourselves together, as is the manner of some, but exhorting one another and so much the more as you see the Day approaching._

According to the previously written verses, name two reasons why we as believers (disciples of Jesus) gather with fellow Christians in church? Write your answers on the lines below.

_____

_____

_____

Why according to Hebrews 5:11-13 was the writer unable to teach deeper truths of God's Word to the believers? Write your answers on the lines below.

_____

_____

_____

_____

Another important element in our spiritual development as disciples of Jesus is the Bible. In 1 Peter 2:1-2, the apostle identifies several things that need to be removed from our lives in order for us to grow as disciples of Jesus. Read the verses and write them down on the lines below. Also, we are to desire the Bible as spiritual food in the same way a baby desires milk. In your own words explain this statement in verse 2.

_____

_____

_____

_____

The Priority of Being a Disciple

In lesson two our focus was the process of becoming a disciple of Jesus Christ, as well as the spiritual development that follows. Here we will consider the price and priority of discipleship. The call to discipleship occurred first during Jesus' ministry upon the earth. While journeying one day through Galilee Jesus saw two brothers: Simon (Peter) and his brother Andrew. Matthew records the call to become His disciples in Matthew 4:19-20 which says: *"Then He said to them, Follow Me, and I will make you fishers of me. They immediately left their nets and followed Him."*

When Jesus uttered the words, **"Follow Me,"** he was calling Peter and Andrew to a new career. They were experienced fishermen and knew how to fish for fish But, He was calling them to become **"fishers of men."** He had a higher calling and a greater task for them. The most important task in the world is that of winning souls. Peter and Andrew were privileged to be the first two persons to receive the call to join Jesus in His work. Since that time He has been issuing the same call to people universally to not only join Him in His work, but also to become His disciples.

Read Mark 1:17 and write on the lines below ways we can join Jesus in His work as **"fishers of men."**

_____

_____

_____

Before we become "**fishers of men**," we must first commit to following Jesus as a disciple. In this case what is involved in being a disciple of Jesus Christ? What price are we to pay? What is the cost? What is the priority of discipleship? In lesson three we will attempt to answer these questions as presented by Jesus in the Scriptures. Let us examine first the terms of *discipleship*. While on His way to Jerusalem to die on the cross, Jesus explained to His disciples the cost of following Him. Luke records His words as follows in Luke 9:23-25:

> *If anyone desires to come after Me, let him deny himself, and take up his cross daily, and follow Me. For whoever desires to save his life will lose it, but whoever loses his life for My sake will save it. For what profit is it to a man if he gains the whole world, and is himself destroyed or lost?*

Many people in the day of Jesus wanted to follow Him, but they wanted to do it on their own terms. However, Jesus says very pointedly "**if anyone desires to come after Me**" (or if anyone desires to be My disciple) these are the terms of discipleship. Here Jesus outlines three primary things all must do if they are to be His disciple. First, he says, "**let him** (everyone) **deny himself.**" What does it mean to deny oneself? The word *deny* commonly used by New Testament writers means "to say not, deny," but the term used by Jesus here is stronger and means "to deny utterly." It is employed only by the Gospel authors and appears in the accounts of Jesus' prediction of Peter's denial of Him (Matthew 26:34-35; Mark 14:30-31; Luke 22:34; John 13:38), and the actual denial of Jesus by Peter (Matthew 26:75; Mark 14:72; Luke 22:61). Simply Jesus wants His disciples to know that He does not offer an easy trip to heaven. It is important to know that He does not mean that we are to create pain or deprivation for ourselves, but as disciples, we are to be prepared to release anything from our lives that is in competition with His kingdom. Simply put in *The Preacher's Outline and Sermon Bible (Luke, p.172)*, as disciples we are not to indulge ourselves in "comfort and ease, appetites and urges, thoughts and feelings, deceptions and enticements, plots and intrigues, pride and boastings, reactions and disturbances." Furthermore, we as disciples of Jesus are to renounce the old life and old self and embrace wholeheartedly the new life and new self along with all the plans and wishes that go with it. That is, we are to say no to self, and yes to Jesus. Additionally, it does not mean to say no to a particular behavior or thing, but to *self*. The idea is to let Christ rule and reign in our hearts and lives, to let Him have His way completely.

Why according to Paul in 2 Corinthians 5:17, are we to embrace the new self and new life? Write your answer on the lines below.

_____

_____

_____

What, according to Paul in Colossians 3:8-12, are we to take off and put on? Write your answers on the lines below.

_____

_____

_____

_____

Second, a devoted follower must "**take up his cross daily.**" The cross was not only for Jesus, but for His disciples as well. The people of Jesus' time had a clear understanding of what it meant to "take up" a cross. Hundreds of criminals had been executed by the Roman government and they witnessed scores of crucifixions. It is important to note that taking up a cross could infer persecution and martyrdom for the disciple of Jesus, however, it does not mean bearing one's particular hardship in life, such as poor health, unemployment, an unsaved spouse, or a wayward child. The cross was always an instrument of death and not an object to carry or bear. According to *The Preacher's Outline and Sermon Bible (Luke)*, the Christian is to possess the same humility of mind as that of Christ, even to the point of death as it pertains to taking up the cross and discipleship (Philippians 2:5-6; 2 Corinthians 10:3-5). He is to put his will, his desires, his wants, his ambitions to death. Additionally, the Christian is to die to the old self and sin and this is to be done *"daily"* which implies continually. Paul expresses this thought about as well as it can be said in Romans 6:11-13. Here he says:

- The believer reckons or counts himself crucified with Christ (Romans 6:6-11).
- The believer reckons or counts himself dead to sin, but alive to God (Romans 6:11).
- The believer does not let sin reign in his body (Romans 6:12).
- The believer does not yield his bodily members as instruments of sin (Romans 6:13a).
- The believer yields himself to God; as much as those who are alive from the dead are yielded to God (Romans 6:13b).
- The believer yields his bodily members as instruments of righteousness (Romans 6:13c).

What does Paul instruct us to do in Romans 12:1 and Colossians 3:5? Write your answers on the lines below.

_____

_____

_____

_____

What does it mean to be a *living sacrifice* in Romans 12:1? Write your answer on the lines provided.

_____

_____

_____

In Galatians 2:20 Paul speaks of being crucified with Christ. In your own words on the lines below write what this means and how does it apply to your life personally.

_____

_____

_____

_____

Third, Jesus said the true disciple must **"follow Me."** The verbs *deny* and *take up* are aorist tense which means that these two acts of Christian discipleship should be a once-for-all and decisive choice that is to be made on a daily basis. But the verb *follow* is present tense, and denotes continuous action. We are on a spiritual journey that will culminate in heaven one day, thus following Jesus on the path He has blazed is to be constant and consistent. Further, the idea of this word is to be a follower or companion of Christ, as well as to be in union with and in the likeness of Christ.

On the lines below write some ways you can follow Jesus in discipleship.

_____

_____

_____

Jesus closes out this section of His teaching on discipleship by saying, **"whoever desires to save his life will lose it, but whoever loses his life for My sake will save it. For what profit is it to a man if he gains the whole world, and is himself destroyed or lost?"** In this part of the passage, Jesus contrasts two kinds of people—who preserve life for self will lose it, while those who lose it for Christ will preserve it. That is, if a disciple spends all his time focusing on this *life* and its fulfillments, he will miss the point entirely of investing for the *life* to come. In his book titled *The Spirit-Anointed Jesus: A Study of the Gospel of Luke*, French Arrington says the word *life* (*psuche*) "refers to the real person." In the context of this passage the warning is stern to all disciples not to invest so much in this earthly life (that passes away, fades, or decays). If a person saves his life, that is, works (lives) to please self on this earth he will lose in eternity or will squander the opportunity to increase his reward in the life that matters most—the eternal kingdom. Note the words, "**for My sake**." The person who works (lives) to please Christ on earth, shall save his life eternally. Arrington, in his commentary, sums up Jesus' teaching by saying that the "loss of position, material things and even physical life" pale in comparison to forfeiting the most important thing—eternal salvation. He goes on to state that we may lose "the wealth, power, and glory the world offers" but we gain true life in Christ both here on earth and in heaven. Further, he points out that it is utter "folly to lose our [eternal] soul over a piece of this world." In essence, the choices that we make now have eternal significance (Luke 9:26).

Read Matthew 16:24-27 and write in your own words on the lines below what it means to deny self, take up the cross, and follow Jesus. How can you do this in your own personal discipleship with Christ?

_____

_____

_____

_____

In the earlier treatment of discipleship (Luke 9:23-25) we learned just how important discipleship is to Jesus, but in this section our focus will be to see how important discipleship should be to us. It is here that we learn the priority of discipleship. Later in this same chapter of Luke we are told that Jesus is continuing His journey toward Jerusalem where He will die as the substitute for humanity's sin (Luke 9:51-56). While making His way toward the city, He encounters three would-be followers. It is at this time Jesus seizes the opportunity to teach the people what is required for wholehearted discipleship. Here in Luke 9:57-62 the overarching truth Jesus reveals is that no special deals or guarantees are offered with regard to discipleship, but that we are to follow Christ, period. That is, we are to be Christ's disciples wherever He leads us and to do whatever He tells us. Further, we are to be committed to Jesus because we love Him for who He is and not for what He can do for us, or for what we can get from Him. Luke writes these words about discipleship in 9:57-62:

Now it happened as they journeyed on the road, that someone said to Him, Lord I will follow You wherever You go. And Jesus said to him, Foxes have holes and birds of the air have nests, but the Son of Man has no where to lay His head. Then He said to another, Follow Me. But He said, Lord, let me first go and bury my father. Jesus said to him, Let the dead bury their own dead, but you go and preach the kingdom of God. And another also said, Lord, I will follow You, but let me first go and bid them farewell who are at my house. But Jesus said to him, No one, having put his hand to the plow, and looking back, is fit for the kingdom of God.

One prospective disciple said, "**I will follow You wherever You go.**" Why would he make such a far-reaching promise? Simply for the same reasons so many people are attracted to Christ today: he enjoyed the Lord's presence and the fellowship with His followers; he was inspired by the teaching and wisdom of Jesus; and he was appreciative of the good deeds Jesus had performed on behalf of others. However, Jesus warned him that there was a cost to be counted and one must be ready to walk the path of self-sacrifice. He said, "**Foxes have holes and birds of the air have nests, but the Son of Man has nowhere to lay His head.**" The essence of Jesus' message here is that there is no guarantee of luxury or material comfort—only self-denial and self-giving. Further, He emphasized the point that following Jesus was to be more than a profession of words, but rather, a priority of action. Additionally, a willingness to follow Jesus is not enough; there must be a commitment to deny oneself, sacrificing, and giving to help meet the needs of others. In essence it is an attitude of service. Thus it is not a self-commitment but rather a commitment to others.

Read Matthew 20:28 and Mark 10:45 and write on the line below why Jesus came.

_____

Read Philippians 2:5-8 and describe on the lines below how Jesus gave of Himself to serve others.

_____

_____

_____

How can you have an attitude of self-service to others? Write your answers on the lines provided.

_____

_____

_____

_____

A second potential disciple of Jesus in this passage was offered an opportunity to follow Him. Jesus extends this invitation to him, **"Follow Me."** Notice how this invitee responds to Jesus' offer to follow Him, **"But He said, Lord let me first go and bury my father."** Jesus in turn says, **"Let the dead bury their own dead, but you go and preach the kingdom of God."** At first the words of Jesus seem a bit cold-hearted, since taking care of one's family needs was paramount among the Jewish people (1 Timothy 5:3-8). This certainly is not the case. What Jesus is really addressing here is delayed obedience to the call of discipleship. His delayed response to the call of discipleship was hampered by divided attention. That is, before he answered the call to become a disciple of Jesus, he wanted first to be free of all other distractions. Further, when he considered the invitation of Jesus, he looked at his circumstance and did not yield immediately. After all, we are talking about the priority of discipleship and there will always be things to distract us in our commitment to Him. Simply said, no person should deny his call to discipleship or delay accepting it. Following Jesus deserves absolute priority. Why was Jesus so insistent that He responded immediately to the call of discipleship? Because the invitation to discipleship has an urgency and mission attached to it—to proclaim the good news of the Gospel so that others may be transformed and blessed.

What does Jesus say in Matthew 6:24 about a disciple's divided loyalty to Him? Write your answer on the following line.

_____

What does 1 John 5:21 teach us about having idols that may distract us in our discipleship? Write your answer on the line below.

Name some ways we may delay an immediate response to the call of Christ to discipleship. Write your answers on the lines below.

_____

_____

_____

_____

The third potential disciple of Jesus in this passage also vowed to follow Him. He said, "**Lord, I will follow You, but let me first go and bid the farewell who are my house.**" Like the previous candidate for discipleship this man was willing to follow Jesus, however, he requested permission to say goodbye to his family. This certainly seemed to be a reasonable request, yet the usage of the words *but* and *first* suggest that he had double allegiance. He made the decision to follow Jesus but something else needed to be handled first—a family affair, a business affair, an employment affair, a financial affair—some other affair was put first as is the case with so many. This prospective disciple by his actions expressed hesitation to cut ties and become a follower of Jesus. There certainly is nothing wrong with our attachment to family but it must not supplant our attachment to Christ. Discipleship is really a priority of relationships. I think the underlying problem with the potential follower of Jesus was not that he wanted to go home, but that he was looking back. Jesus must have discerned that because His next comments were a warning against looking back. To illustrate His point Jesus used the metaphor of plowing. He said, "**No one, having put his hand to the plow, and looking back, is fit for the kingdom of God.**" Jesus was simply saying that any disciple who begins walking on the path of discipleship and looks back is not fit for the kingdom of God. Why would Jesus make such a stringent statement? He made this statement because He understood that no one could plow consistently while looking back over his shoulder. In other words, following Jesus calls for devotion and concentration. Further, when a disciple looks back it distracts him from giving wholehearted service or his very best to the Lord.

What does Matthew 6:33 teach about the place God should have in our lives? Write your answer on the following lines.

_____

_____

_____

When we put God first in our lives what promise does God make to us according to Matthew 6:33? Write your answer on the lines below.

_____

_____

_____

In Colossians 3:2 Paul says the affections of disciples are to be focused on what? Write your answer on the lines below.

_____

_____

_____

In Luke 14, Jesus and His followers are continuing their journey toward Jerusalem. Soon He would face a Roman cross and be crucified as the Lamb of God to take away the sin of the world (John 1:29). As they traveled together Jesus used the time to teach about the demands of discipleship. His primary point of emphasis is that discipleship is not cheap and does cost. Dietrich Bonhoeffer, the German theologian, in his great book *The Cost of Discipleship*, expressed these thoughts on the demands of discipleship. He wrote:

> *Cheap grace is grace without discipleship, grace without the cross, grace without Jesus Christ, living and incarnate . . . Costly grace is the treasure hidden in the field; for the sake*

of it a man will gladly go and sell all that he has. It is costly because it costs a man his life, and it is grace because it gives a man the only true life.

Luke 14: 25-35 is a passage where Jesus addresses the cost of discipleship. It is here that he turns to the massive crowd of people following Him and says, **"If anyone comes to Me," or "if anyone wants to be My disciple"** . . . these are the demands that apply to everyone who wants to be My disciple. First, He said, there is a cost in relationships as stated in Luke 14:26. It says, *If anyone comes to Me and does not hate his father and mother, and wife and children, brothers and sisters, yes, and his own life also, he cannot be My disciple.*

On the surface this seems to be a really harsh statement by Jesus and contrary to His teaching on love elsewhere. Did He really mean that we are to *hate* those closest to us in order to be His disciple? To understand what Jesus meant by this statement we need to explore the definition of the word *hate.* The term does not mean that we are to literally hate those closest to us, nor should we have feelings of aversion or malice. Even believers are commanded to love their enemies (Luke 6:27). The idea behind this requirement for discipleship is that no other relationship we have should transcend our relationship with Christ. In essence Jesus wants our relationship with Him to be more important than any other intimate relationships we may have. Further, in the words of Tony Evans in his book, *What Matters Most,* "there is to be nothing in my life that deserves my commitment, my determination, and my passions more than my love for Christ." Additionally, a writer in *The Preacher's Outline and Sermon Bible (Luke)* summed up this directive about discipleship in this manner. He wrote:

- Christ is to be first in a person's life: before family, even before self.

- Christ is to be put before family: even if one's family opposes his decision to follow Christ.

- Christ is to be put first: before the companionship and comfort and pleasure of family and home.

- All—even family and self—are to be put behind Christ and His mission.

What does Jesus say in Matthew 10:37 with regard to our relationship with Him? Write your answer on the lines below.

_____

_____

What does Jesus teach in Matthew 22: 37-38 about how we should love God? Write your answers on the following lines.

_____

_____

_____

_____

_____

Second, Luke states that there is a cost in being identified with Jesus. Luke 14: 27 states: "*And whoever does not bear his cross and come after Me cannot be My disciple.*"

What does it mean to "**bear [carry] his cross**?" When a criminal was sentenced to die by crucifixion, that person was ordered by the Roman Empire to carry his cross part of the way to the crucifixion site. Carrying a cross through the city was a declaration that Rome was correct in imposing the death sentence upon him, as well as an admission that he was wrong and Rome was right. As it relates to discipleship, Jesus enjoins His followers to carry their cross in the same way as a means of publicly identifying with Him. It is a daily identification with Christ in shame, suffering, and surrender to God's will. It further means death to self, to our own plans and ambitions, and a willingness to serve Him as He directs.

In John 12:23-28 what does Jesus teach say about following Him? Write your answer on the following lines.

_____

_____

_____

_____

The "cross" is something we willingly accept from God and the message Jesus conveys here is "I want you to carry your cross through town" (wherever you go). That is, He wants our identification with Him to be so publicly displayed that when we are accused of being a Christian (disciple), we say, "I'm guilty as charged." It is a call to be on public display, to be identified with Jesus in every area of our life. Another thing that needs to be considered here is that when a person was sentenced to die by crucifixion, it was a one-way journey. He was going to die and there was no turning around. Very simply, when Jesus calls us to be a disciple, He "bids us to come and die."

When Jesus says in Mark 8:38 that we should not be ashamed of Him, what does He mean? Write your answer on the lines provided.

_____

_____

_____

What are the consequences of being ashamed of Jesus in this life? Write your answer on the lines provided.

_____

_____

_____

Third, Luke declares in chapter 14 that discipleship is a deliberative choice. That is, one must give thought to discipleship; he must count the cost and the consequences. Jesus uses two parables to illustrate His point. These parables are found in Luke 14:28-32: the first is that of a builder who wants to construct a tower; and the second, is a king who is contemplating going to war. We will consider these parables separately in our study. Let us look first at the parable of the builder which is found in Luke 14:28-30 and says:

> _For which of you, intending to build a tower, does not sit down first and count the cost, whether he has enough to finish it—lest, after he has laid the foundation, and is not able to finish, all who see it begin to mock him._

Here Jesus says it is necessary to count the cost of discipleship. In essence, salvation is a free gift of God's grace (Romans 3:24; 6:23; Ephesians 2:8-9), but discipleship is costly. In other words, the call to discipleship is a serious matter and the choice to follow Jesus is not to be taken flippantly, but wholeheartedly. Consequently, before committing ourselves to follow Jesus, we must take out our spiritual calculators and add up the cost to see if we have sufficient resources to follow through and finish, not just start. The point is clear: Christ wants anyone who considers being His disciple to first sit down and think about it.

In the second parable Jesus speaks of two kings that are contemplating going to war against each other. Luke 14:31-32 states:

> _Or what king, going to make war against another king, does not sit down first and consider whether he is able with ten thousand to meet him who comes against him with twenty thousand? Or else, while the other is still a great way off, he sends a delegation and asks conditions of peace._

In similar fashion Jesus says, "in order to be My disciple one must first count the cost" (paraphrased). This story tells of one king who is deliberating about going to war with another king who has launched an attack against him. Before so doing, he must sit down and consciously think about what the cost of such an action would be to him and his army. Thus the defending king had to think about the prospects of loss of life, as well as the loss of property if he engaged the enemy in war. Would it be worth the cost? Note: the king had a decision to make. The point of the parable is that there can be no neutrality in following Christ. Either we do or we don't. Everyone must make a decision. One just can't sit idly by and be a disciple of Jesus.

How did Moses challenge the Hebrew nation to not be neutral in their relationship with God in Exodus 32:26? Write you answer on the lines below.

_____

_____

_____

How did Elijah challenge the people of Israel in 1 Kings 18:21 about being divided in their commitment to God? Write your answer on the lines below.

_____

_____

_____

In summary, the first parable teaches that a person is not to blindly become a disciple of Jesus, but should consider whether or not he or she can afford to follow Him. Whereas, the second story instructs us to think about the cost of *not following Jesus* and that we are to come to terms with the stronger enemy (Satan) as we are engaged in a spiritual war with eternal consequences.

How does 1 Peter 5:8 characterize Satan as our enemy? Write your answer on the lines below.

_____

_____

How does Paul say that we can prepare ourselves to fight against Satan and his spiritual forces in Ephesians 6:10-17? Write your answers on the lines below.

_____

_____

_____

_____

Jesus adds one last point to His teaching on the cost of discipleship and it is found in verse 33 where He says: *So likewise, whoever of you does not forsake all that he has cannot be My disciple.*

The message is quite clear: no person can be the disciple of Christ unless he forsakes all and follows Him. When a person considers being a disciple of Jesus it will cost him all he is and all he has. In *The Preacher's Outline and Sermon Bible (Luke),* the author says it will cost man:

- His heart: total devotion and commitment.
- His mind: being permeated and controlled by Christ.
- His eyes: watching what he looks at.
- His ears: watching what he listens to.
- His hands: watching what he touches and picks up.
- His feet: watching where he goes.
- His mouth: watching what he says.
- His desires: watching, controlling, and changing his urges.
- His energy: committing his strength, initiative, and his will to Christ.

Further, a person desiring to be Jesus' disciple must be willing to surrender all he has to Christ. The term *forsake* when used with reference to persons, carries the idea of taking leave of or saying goodbye to someone, however, when employed with regard to things (possessions), it means to give up or renounce. This is the meaning of the word in verse 33. Jesus is not indicating that a disciple necessarily is to sell all his or her possessions and give everything away, but rather we are to surrender them to Christ, and He will in turn trust us as His stewards with the things He owns.

Compare the reaction of the rich young ruler in Luke 18:18-30 to this demand of discipleship and write on the lines below how he failed to meet it.

_____

_____

_____

_____

_____

Think about your own life for a moment and ask yourself: Is there anything that I am withholding from the Lord that is hindering me in my personal discipleship? Write it on the lines below if you can identify any specific thing.

_____

_____

_____

In verses 34-35, Jesus closes the discourse by warning those who potentially want to be His disciples against following Him halfheartedly and failing to count the cost of discipleship. He states:

> *Salt is good; but if the salt has lost its flavor, how shall it be seasoned? It is neither fit for the land nor for the dunghill (rubbish heap), but men throw it out. He who has ears to hear, let him hear!*

Jesus emphatically says here that those who fail to take the demands of discipleship seriously are comparable to "saltless" salt. Therefore, they lose their effectiveness and can't be used by the Lord in kingdom ministry. Further, when one lacks the true qualities of discipleship (loving the Lord supremely, carrying the cross daily, and deliberately counting the cost) they are completely following the Lord. Jesus concludes, **"he who has ears to hear, let him hear!"** In other words, we are to be spiritually attuned to what the Lord is saying about the price and priority of discipleship. Otherwise we cannot be His disciples.

The Productivity of a Disciple

In our last lesson of this discipleship study, we will explore John 15 which is part of Jesus' final discourse with His disciples. It is in this passage (John 15:1-27) that Jesus instructs His followers on three vital relationships. He says: disciples are to be rightly related to Him (vv.1-10), to each other (vv.11-17), and to the world (vv. 18-27). The first of these relationships is primary for our study. Presented here in John 15 is the profile and productivity of a disciple. Bill Hull, in his classic study titled *The Disciple-Making Pastor* identifies six specific profiles of the disciple of Christ. The list is as follows:

- A Disciple Remains in Christ (15:7)
- A Disciple is Obedient (15:9)
- A Disciple Bears Fruit (15:8, 16)
- A Disciple Glorifies God (15:8)
- A Disciple Has Joy (15:11)
- A Disciple Loves as Christ Loves (15:12-14,17)

Throughout our examination of John 15 some of these profile characteristics will be alluded to; however, more emphasis will be placed on the ultimate purpose for being a disciple of Jesus Christ, which is to produce fruit. Jesus begins this necessary teaching on discipleship with the Gospel's final "I am" statement (6:35; 8:12; 10:9; 11-25-26; 14:6).

Read the listed references for Jesus' other "I am" statements and write them on the lines below. Give a brief explanation of each in your own words.

_____

_____

_____

_____

_____

_____

In earlier sayings, the focus of Jesus was describing Himself as the life-giver and with each came an invitation to "come to Him," however, here He is speaking directly to those who have already responded to the invitation and are in the process of developing as disciples of Jesus Christ. His primary point of emphasis is that the disciples must remain in relationship with him. To illustrate His point, Jesus utilizes a common image very familiar to them—the vine and its branches. He begins by saying, *I am the true vine, and My Father is the vinedresser* (John 15:1). What prompted Jesus to use the illustration of the vine is certainly open to conjecture; however, it is believed that He uttered these words somewhere between the Upper Room and the Garden of Gethsemane. Some have theorized that as they passed the Temple, Jesus caught glimpse of its gates, which were made of bronze and had shaped into it a golden vine. It is likely that His familiarity with the Old Testament proved as a source of knowledge as well. It is there that Israel is viewed with the same imagery as indicated by multiple references. First, there is Psalm 80:8-9, which states:

> *You have brought a vine out of Egypt; You have cast out the nations, and planted it.*
> *You prepared room for it, and caused it to take deep root, and it filled the land.*

Jeremiah continues with the same symbolic reference to Israel with two separate statements as found in the following verses of Jeremiah 2:21; and 6:9 which state:

> *Yet I had planted you a noble vine, a seed of the highest quality, how then have you turned before Me into the degenerate plant of an alien vine?*

> *Thus says the Lord of hosts: "They shall thoroughly glean as a vine the remnant of Israel; as a grape-gatherer, put your hand back into the branches."*

However, the most recognized of these vine, or vineyard references that apply to Israel is found in what has been termed as *The Song of the Vineyard* as written in the words of Isaiah in 5:1-2, 7:

> *Now let me sing to my Well-beloved a song of my Beloved regarding His vineyard: My Well-beloved has a vineyard on a very fruitful hill. He dug it up and cleared out its stones, and planted it with the choicest vine. He built a tower in its midst, and also made a winepress in it; So He expected it to bring forth good grapes, But it brought forth wild grapes . . . For the vineyard of the Lord of hosts is the house of Israel, and the men of Judah are His pleasant plant. He looked for justice, but behold, oppression; For righteousness, but behold, a cry for help.*

The picture in each verse shows Israel to be a degenerate vine with dried-up fruit, and a withered vine consumed with fire (Ezekiel 19:12) when she should have been "the choicest vine" bringing "forth grapes" (Isaiah 5:2). It is against this backdrop that Jesus uses the symbol **I am the true vine**. This metaphor is now expanded to include all believers and is individualized in its application. What does Jesus mean when He says, "**I am the true vine**?" The word for *true* here is *alethinos*, which means "genuine." J. Vernon McGee in his commentary *Thru the Bible* (John 11-21), states that a thing can be true as over against error and falsehood, or a thing can be true over against that which is counterfeit. The latter definition best fits the context of our study passage. Two other times in the Gospel of John this word is used in the same way. First, John the Baptist was a reflecting light, but Jesus is the true Light (1:6-9), and the second occurrence draws a contrast between the bread given by Moses in the wilderness, but Jesus Christ is the true Bread (6:22-33). As the term is applied to Jesus in this context it draws a comparison between Him and Israel and the message is that identifying with the Jewish nation and Jewish religion is not the essential thing. He simply says, "I am the genuine or real vine" and if you are going to be a fruit-bearing disciple then you must be properly related to me. You must have a relationship with me. You must be connected to me. Furthermore, it is not one's identification with a particular religious system or organization that matters most, but rather one's identification with Jesus Christ that is essential. After making this revolutionary statement Jesus went on to say that "**my Father is the vinedresser**." This, too, was a shocking thought because in most Old Testament passages God is viewed as the owner of the vineyard. The term **vinedresser** in this specific context could be translated "farmer," "gardener" or "one who keeps or cares for the vineyard."

The picture given here by John is that the Father is responsible for tending, watering, cultivating, and protecting the vineyard so that it can produce the proper kind of fruit. This reaches back to the Old Testament and Isaiah's first vineyard song, where God is depicted as tending His vineyard, only to be rewarded with sour grapes (Isaiah 5:1-7).

In verse one of this important chapter on discipleship, John identifies for us the roles of Jesus and the Father in developing disciples as fruit-bearers; however, beginning with verses two through eleven, the writer speaks more specifically about the process used by the Father to form us into productive disciples, as well as the kind of relationship we are to have with Christ (the vine), if we (the branches), are to produce spiritual fruit. At the outset of this portion of the study it is important to ask, "What is fruit?" It is important to note that Jesus mentions the word *fruit* six times in the first 10 verses. Generally speaking most equate "fruit" to that of winning others to Christ because in Romans 1:13 Paul states, *Now I do not want you to be unaware, brethren, that I often planned to come to you . . . that I might have some fruit among you also, just as among the other Gentiles.* While winning others to Christ certainly is spiritual fruit, however, Bruce Wilkinson, in his book *Secrets of the Vine* indicates that fruit could be used interchangeably with good works, which represents a thought, attitude, or action in our lives that brings glory to God. That's why Jesus states, "By this [fruit-bearing] My Father is glorified, that you bear much fruit; so you will be My disciples" (John 15:8). Paul in his writings supports the same idea (Ephesians 2:10; Titus 2:14).

Read Ephesians 2:10 and Titus 2:14 and explain in your own words on the lines below what it means to have good works in our lives.

_____

_____

_____

_____

_____

Paul further adds that we bear inward and outward fruit. Outward fruit is when we allow God to nurture certain qualities within us, while outward fruit is when we permit God to work through us.

Read Galatians 5:22 and write on the lines below the kind of inward fruit that is produced in our lives.

_____

_____

_____

Read 2 Corinthians 9:8 and write on the lines how God enables us to produce outward fruit (works) in our lives.

_____

_____

_____

Read Matthew 25:31-40 and identify ways we can produce outward works (fruit) on the lines below.

_____

_____

_____

_____

The importance and value of our fruit-bearing as disciples is stated by Jesus in John 15:16 where he says, "You did not choose Me, but I chose you and appointed you that you should go and bear fruit, and that you fruit remain . . ." (NKJV). Simply put, our fruit is the only permanent deposit we have in heaven. In other words, real fruit lasts! (15:16). And according to Paul in Ephesians

2:10, it's the main earthly reason we were saved. He says that "we are His workmanship created in Christ Jesus for good works which God prepared beforehand that we should walk in them."

Now that we understand Jesus' primary purpose for every disciple is to produce good works (fruit), let's consider the process initiated by God to help us reach our maximum potential as fruit-bearing contributors to His program in the world. Bruce Wilkinson, in his text titled *Secrets of the Vine* says that Jesus identifies four levels of fruit-bearers in John 15.

- "No fruit" (v.2)
- "Fruit" (v.2)
- "More fruit" (v.2)
- "Much fruit" (v.5)

The goal of every disciple is to reach level four ("much fruit"). How do we reach the level of "much fruit?" One step in the process of becoming an optimum fruit-bearer for Christ is stated by Jesus in John 15:2 which states: *Every branch in Me that does not bear fruit He takes away; and every branch that bears fruit He prunes, that it may bear more fruit.*

Notice that Jesus is directing these words to those "**in Me**" which speaks of the persons who are already "in Christ." The indication here is that those being addressed by Jesus have an organic relationship with Him; that is, they are genuine believers at different levels of their spiritual development. The goal of Jesus is to move each one from *just* a relationship with Him to a *more* intimate fellowship with Him through the *process* of discipleship. Each vineyard is to produce fruit and it is the gardener's responsibility to ensure that this happens. Jesus states here that the branches that do not produce fruit, the gardener "**takes away**" (cuts off) those who do not bear fruit and for those who do bear fruit He "**prunes**." These two activities are seen according to some scholars in John 13, with the cutting off of Judas (13:21-30) and the cleansing of the disciples (13:10). However, for the purpose of this study a different definition can be used and is best suited for the particular context. The first phrase *takes away* can better be translated "to lift up" or "to take up." Several examples of this definition are found in other New Testament references. For example, it is used in Matthew 14:20 when the disciples took up 12 baskets of food following the miracle of Jesus feeding the multitudes. Other references include when Simon was compelled to "bear" the cross of Jesus (Matthew 27:32), and when Jesus is called the Lamb of God that "takes away" the sin of the world by John the Baptist (John 1:29). But, how does this apply to discipleship? To understand one has to have knowledge of vineyards in the Middle East, and how some would lie on the ground not getting enough sunlight, as well as being covered with too much dirt. Without the proper sunlight and being dirty, that particular branch would not produce the necessary fruit. That the case, the keeper of the vineyard would come by and "lift up" the branch, wash off the dirt, tie it to a post or pole, and then the branch would become productive in bearing fruit. There are two primary ways God, the vinedresser, accomplishes the task of lifting up and washing the branch. First, if the branch is not productive in bearing fruit the gardener (God) employs discipline. Regarding the disciplinary actions used, the writers of Hebrews give us insight. He says, "My son, do not despise the chastening (discipline) of the Lord, nor be discouraged when you are rebuked by Him; For whom the Lord loves He chastens (disciplines), And scourges every son whom He receives" (Hebrews 12:5-6).

Read Hebrews 12:5-6 and write on the lines below three methods that God disciplines unfruitful branches. Explain each method in your own words.

_____

_____

_____

_____

God's goal in disciplining us is that we may become fruitful, productive branches.

Read Hebrews 12:11 and write on the lines below the goal God has in disciplining His children.

_____

_____

_____

_____

In addition to discipline being God's proactive answer for moving barren branches to fruitfulness, He also employs the procedure of purging or pruning to increase the fruit-bearing ability of those branches that are productive. The goal is to produce more fruit. Bruce Wilkinson, in his book _Secrets of the Vine_ shows the importance of the pruning process by saying that "the vine's ability to produce growth increases each year, but without intensive pruning the plant weakens and its crop diminishes. Mature branches must be pruned hard to achieve maximum yields." The word "**prunes**" in this verse means "to trim" or "to cleanse." While there are multiple ways God can prune the branches for optimum production, there are two primary means that come to mind. First, He prunes us through the testing of our faith. This method of pruning His people is recognized and recorded in both the Old and New Testaments. Consider the words of Psalm 66:12, which states: "We went through fire and through water; but You brought us out to rich fulfillment (abundance)." James adds: "My brethren, count it all joy when you fall into various trials, knowing that the testing of your faith produces patience. But let patience have its perfect work, that you may be perfect and complete, lacking nothing" (1:2-4). Peter continues this line of thought with his words in 1 Peter 1: 6-7 which says, "In this you greatly rejoice, though now for a little while, if need be, you have been grieved by various trials, that the genuineness of your faith, being much more precious than gold that perishes, though it be tested by fire, may be found to praise, honor, and glory at the revelation of Jesus Christ."

Read all the above verses (Psalm 66:12; James 1:2-4; and 1 Peter 1:6-7) and write in your own words on the lines below how God uses "the testing of our faith" to increase our productivity as fruit-bearing disciples.

_____

_____

_____

_____

_____

_____

_____

_____

Second, God prunes disciples through the Word of God. Notice the words of Jesus in John 15:3. He says: *"You are already clean because of the word which I have spoken to you."*

Jesus' disciples have been cleansed by His word. The term *word* derives from a Greek word *logos* and implies His entire teaching or message to this point in their spiritual development. Of course, the disciples of that time did not have the complete canon of Scripture and I think He is making reference to the Word of God serving as a cleansing agent in the future as well. After all, later in this final discourse, Jesus prior to death on the cross would pray: "Sanctify them by Your truth. Your word is truth" (John 17:17). The words of Jesus' prayer not only applied to His present disciples, but also to those who believe on Him in future generations. Thus the Word of God would not only serve as a cleansing agent for disciples of Jesus' day, it would act as one in our time as well. This is clear from other Biblical references as well. Throughout the Old and New Testaments the writers show how important God's Word is in our lives as disciples.

Read 1 Peter 1:23 and write on the lines below the role God's Word plays in our conversion experience.

_____

_____

_____

_____

Read Psalm 119:9 and write on the lines below how we as disciples maintain a pure lifestyle before God.

_____

_____

_____

_____

God's Word is a deterrent to sin when we do what according to Psalm 119:11? Read this verse and write your answer on the lines below.

_____

_____

_____

_____

_____

Read James 1:22 and write on the lines below what we are to do and what we are not to do with regard to God's Word in our lives.

_____

_____

_____

_____

Read James 1:23-24 and write on the lines below how the apostle describes a person who is only a hearer of God's Word and not a practitioner of God's Word.

_____

_____

_____

_____

Above we discussed the process used by the Father to increase our effectiveness as fruit-bearing disciples of Christ; however, as we move forward in the study of John 15 focus will be on the thought of our connectivity as a branch to the vine. Simply, Jesus says that unless you stay connected to Me you will not be a maximum producer of fruit in your Christian life. John 15:4-5 describes it in this manner:

> *Abide in Me, and I in you. As the branch cannot bear fruit of itself, unless it abides in the vine, neither can you, unless you abide in Me. I am the vine, you are the branches. He who abides in Me, and I in him, bears much fruit; for without Me you can do nothing.*

Key in this section is the term ***abide***. Within six verses of John 15 Jesus employs this word at least ten times. In fact, John uses the word around 40 times in the Gospel, and 68 times throughout his writings. Additionally, it appears 118 times in the New Testament. The term derives from a Greek verb *meno* and means "to remain or stay," such as someone staying in a specific location (Matthew 26:38; John 1:38-39), town (John 7:9; Acts 9:43), or house (Matthew 10:11; Luke 19:5). Yet as Jesus uses the word here it involves more of a spiritual significance referring to some aspect of our relationship with God, which is also the case of its 24 occurrences in 1 John. *Meno* carries the idea of staying in a relationship that has already begun or continuing a process already started. The chief passage where we find this usage of the word is John 15:1-16 and here Jesus addresses specifically the continuation of a disciples' relationship with Him if they are to be optimum bearers of spiritual fruit. In addition it is important to note that the word ***abide*** appears in the form of a command or imperative—not a recommendation or option. Hence if branches (disciples) are to be maximum bearers of spiritual fruit they must stay connected to the vine (Him). Bruce Wilkinson in *Secrets of the Vine* sums it up in this manner: "If your life bears a lot of fruit, God will invite you to abide more deeply with Him." So Jesus states that He is "the vine" and disciples are "the branches" and says, "**Abide in Me, and I in you**"… but adds, "**for without Me you can do nothing**." This phrase means "separated from me [Christ] you cannot bear fruit." He is not implying that we cannot be successful in performing our daily routines, or accomplishing tasks that are before us; however, the meaning is that apart from a vital, continual, and ongoing relationship with Him we cannot produce the right kind of spiritual fruit in our Christian life. Additionally, as one writer puts it: "the fruit that disciples bear is not what they do, but the life of Jesus in them. It is His character reproduced within them and shared with others in love. This cannot come to pass without the disciple abiding in Jesus, making His home in Him as Jesus makes His home in the disciple. His life is shared with the disciples as their life is given [submitted] to Him." Commenting further on the disciples' responsibility of maintaining a continual relationship with Christ in order to bear spiritual fruit another writer adds: "Remaining is not simply believing in him, though, that is crucial, but includes being in union with him, sharing his thoughts, emotions, intentions and power. In a relationship both parties must be engaged. The divine must take the initiative and provide the means and the ability for the union to take place, but it cannot happen without the response of the disciple." Thus the key term "abiding" used with regularity throughout the discourse (115:4-7,9,10) reveals that the growing disciple in whom the Father and Son live (14:20,23) through the Spirit (14:16, 25; 15:26) is one whose life is completely dependent on Christ. That is, discipleship is not just a matter of acknowledging who Jesus is, it is having Jesus spiritually connected to our inner lives. Jesus further adds a serious warning to those who fail to "abide" in Him. He states in verse 6: *If anyone does not abide in Me, he is cast out as a branch and is withered; and they gather them and throw them into the fire, and they are burned.*

But what is meant by the words ***he is cast out as a branch and is withered; and they gather them and throw them into the fire, and they are burned***? There are some who think this is a reference to the eschatological judgment of hell (Matthew 3:10; 7:19; Mark 9:43; Luke 3:9; John 5:29) for those who do not remain in the Vine (Jesus), and it is clear from this verse that Christ did not believe "once in the vine, always in the vine." Furthermore, this parable teaches that it is indeed possible for true believers to abandon faith, and turn their backs on Jesus. While this understanding of verse 6 is possible; however, the immediate context seems to suggest that disciples who fail to maintain a constant relationship with Christ, or who do not continue to "abide in Christ" lose their effectiveness as witnesses for Christ, and their ability to produce spiritual fruit. Thus they are like wood that is brittle and good for nothing but to be used as fuel for a fire. Jesus seems to draw from the imagery of Ezekiel 15:1-8 where the people of Jerusalem are compared to a branch that does not bear spiritual fruit, and is therefore useless. Simply put, apart from staying connected to Jesus through an ongoing relationship we will be barren in our spiritual productivity, and therefore, useless in Kingdom ministry.

Read Ezekiel 15:1-8 and write in your own words on the lines below the reasons why Israel was not a fruitful branch for God. Compare it to what Jesus is saying in John 15 and identify any similarities with modern day disciples of Christ.

_____

_____

_____

_____

Read 1 Corinthians 3:10-15 and write on the lines below why it is important to build our lives as Christian believers on the right foundation. Also write how God will judge the works of believers in the future as well.

_____

_____

_____

_____

In John 15:1-6, Jesus has discussed how vital it is for disciples to stay connected to Him through an ongoing relationship if they are to be productive bearers of spiritual fruit. However, in verse 7, the focus changes to necessary keys that keep us connected to the vine as branches. They are twofold: being rightly related to the words of Christ; and being committed to Christ through prayer. Listen to Jesus as He speaks: *If you abide in Me, and My words abide in you, you will ask what you desire, and it shall be done for you.*

It is important to note that this verse begins with the conditional word *If* which clearly indicates that maintaining a vital relationship with Jesus is entirely the choice of each disciple. Daily a disciple must choose: "Will I follow Christ today or will I remain in relationship with Christ today?" If a disciple chooses to continually remain in Christ then they must first allow His words (the Scriptures) to "**abide**" in them. In other words, the disciple must have a commitment to the Scriptures. That is, the "**words of Christ**" must have an integral place in their lives.

Read John 8:31 and write on the lines below what Jesus says about the His teachings and discipleship.

_____

_____

_____

_____

Read Colossians 3:16 and write in your own words on the lines below what you think Paul means by the phrase "let the word of Christ dwell in you richly"?

_____

_____

_____

_____

Read 2 Timothy 2:15 and explain in your own words on the lines below why we should do our best in studying the Scriptures. What does Paul mean when he says "rightly dividing the word of truth"? Write your answer below.

_____

_____

_____

_____

_____

Read 1 Peter 3:15 and write in your own words on the lines below why it is important for us to be prepared to give an answer for the hope within us.

_____

_____

_____

_____

Additionally, if a disciple chooses daily to remain in Christ there must be a commitment to prayer. Jesus says, "**you will ask what you desire, and it shall be done for you.**" Contrary to popular belief among some this verse does not give a disciple "carte blanche." It must be balanced with other Scriptural teaching and qualifications on prayer.

Read 1 John 3:22 and write on the lines below what qualification is mentioned as a condition for answered prayer.

_____

_____

_____

_____

Read 1 John 5:14-15 and write on the lines below how John says we are to pray as a condition to answered prayer.

_____

_____

Notice also in this verse that Jesus adds a condition to being effective in our prayer life. He says, " **if you abide in Me, and My words abide in you**." That is, apart from remaining continually in Christ and having His words constantly dwelling in us an effective prayer life is just not possible. In essence prayer (communication with God) becomes the basis for remaining (abiding) in Christ and is the root of living as a disciple for Christ. Simply put, God talks to us through the

Scriptures and by prayer we talk back to Him. Jesus closes His teaching on bearing spiritual fruit with the words of John 15:8 which state: "**By this My Father is glorified, that you bear much fruit; so you will be My disciples.**" Not only are we to produce spiritual fruit as a disciple, our fruit is to remain for that is the chief purpose Jesus chose us as is indicated in John 15:16: "**You did not choose Me, but I chose you and appointed you that you should go forth and bear fruit, and that your fruit should remain, that whatever you ask the Father in My name He may give you.**"

Read John 15:12-17 and write on the lines below how disciples are to relate to each other.

_____

_____

_____

_____

Read John 15: 18-25 and write on the lines below how disciples are to relate to the world.

_____

_____

_____

_____

_____

_____

_____

_____

Conclusion

The express purpose of this study has been to explore and explain basic tenets of Christian discipleship. The journey began with the Great Commission given by Christ in Matthew 28 to "make disciples" and concluded in John 15 with a brief explanation of the profile and productivity of a disciple. It is important to understand that before we can "make disciples" we must first become a disciple. I am reminded of the words of Jesus in Mark 1:17, which state: **"Follow Me, and I will make you become fishers of men**." Notice the sequence: discipleship (follow) and then make disciples (fishers of men). In between, we learned that the process of becoming a disciple of Christ enjoins each of us to take upon our life His yoke and learn of Him. Also, we explored that in order to be a disciple of Christ He must have supreme priority in a our life, and, no other relationship we have is to supplant the one we have with Him. In summary, the chief purpose for being a disciple of Christ is to produce spiritual fruit, and the evidence of that fruit should remain. We close with these words of Jesus: **"Therefore by their fruits you will know them"** (Matthew 7:20).

Bibliography

Arrington, French L. *The Spirit-Anointed Jesus: A Study of the Gospel of Luke.*
    Cleveland, Tenn.: Pathway Press, 2008.

Bonhoeffer, Dietrich. *The Cost of Discipleship.* New York: MacMillan Publishing, 1997.

Culpepper, Raymond F. *The Great Commission: The Solution.* Cleveland, Tenn.:
    Pathway Press, 2009.

Evans, Tony. *What Matters Most: Four Absolute Necessities for Following Christ.*
    Chicago: Moody Press, 1997.

_____. *What a Way to Live: Running All of Life by the Kingdom Agenda.*
    Nashville, Tenn.: Word Publishing, 1997.

Holman Christian Standard Study Bible. Nashville, Tenn.: Holman Bible Publishers,
    2010.

Hull, Bill. *The Disciple-Making Pastor.* Grand Rapids, Michigan: Fleming H. Revell,
    1999.

McGee, J. Vernon. *Thru the Bible Commentary Series: John Chapters 11-21.* Nashville,
    Tenn.: Thomas Nelson, 1995.

Preacher's Outline and Sermon Bible: Luke. Vol.4 2nd ed. Chattanooga, Tenn.: Alpha-
    Omega Ministries, 1996.

Wilkinson, Bruce. *Secrets of the Vine.* Sisters, Oregon: Multnomah Press, 2001.

Willis, Avery T., Jr., Moore, Kay. *The Disciple's Cross: MasterLife.* Nashville, Tenn.:
    LifeWay Press, 2009.

SECTION 13

MINISTRY OF ASSIMILATION

A PROCESS TO HELP PEOPLE FIND THEIR PLACE

IN YOUR CHURCH.

LARRY L. EVANS

SECTION 13

HELPING PEOPLE FIND THEIR PLACE

The vision for this ministry plan

The vision for this assimilation ministry is for your church to become a place where new individuals can experience love, acceptance, and care from the moment they walk in the doors to the time they exit. And to set up a consistent follow-up plan that will effectively provide the new individual with a sense of belonging. Ultimately to provide the new individual with a sense of empowerment by encouraging him/her to excel in their personal ministry gifts as they are integrated and brought through the various levels of commitment to the Church.

The starting point: Outreach.

Before guests ever arrive they will have heard something or met someone that motivated them to come and check out one of your church services. Here is an extensive list on how you could reach them.

Events (some listed are larger and more costly, but reaching far more people—often city-wide events, but also community-specific events). Examples include:

1.   Festivals (e.g. kids programming, moon bounces, etc.).

2.   Cosponsor large community events (partnering with local communities and civic organizations).

3.   Free community skating party.

4.   Special 9/11 Memorial Service.

5.   Celebrity Golf Tournament.

6.   Public-servant recognition day (for police, fireman, military etc.).

7.   Free family movie nights (with popcorn and drinks).

8.   Free concerts (series of summer evening concerts).

9.   Vacation Bible School (or Backyard Vacation Bible School in numerous homes).

10.   Community/neighborhood cookouts and block parties.

11.   Sporting tournaments (e.g. 3 on 3 basketball tournament, flag football league, fishing tournaments etc.).

12.   Sponsor classic car show.

13. Special services (Easter production, Christmas Eve service, Community New Year's Eve party, Fireworks on the fourth of July).

14. Parents' night out (fun activities for kids at local church while parents go out).

These types of events will typically take more effort, coordination and money than service projects but they will reach more people. In identifying events, consider researching local community/city and neighborhood association plans. Look for ways to partner/participate in events already planned by the community.

Classes/Seminars (typically these activities target specific demographics within the community and center upon the needs of the targeted group—can target large or small groups of people).

Examples include:

1. Parenting seminar.

2. Newcomers Guide to the Community (practical seminar to get new people in the community familiar with the services and features of the community—this would work well with new students coming into a local university).

3. Marriage workshop.

4. Personal finances/budgeting workshop.

5. Time management workshop.

6. Basic computer skills.

7. Job interview and resume skills.

8. Basic landscaping seminar.

> The key to prioritizing classes and seminars is to ask, "Who will we reach?" "How big is the felt need (i.e. how many people is this likely to appeal to)?" "Where will the class be held?" and "Who will lead it (i.e. get a community leader with credibility—the local high school principal to lead a parenting seminar)?" Get innovative. Use these seminars to network in the community. The best contacts you make may be in finding seminar leaders and facility locations.

Service Opportunities, which are typically smaller in scale and low cost—usually target localized groups of people).[1] Service opportunities are almost endless and include:

1. Adopt a highway for cleanup.

2. Volunteer service at local schools.

3. Car wash.

4. Pumping gas and car window washing.

5. Carrying groceries to cars.

6. Giving away bottled water to commuters.

7. Giving away stamps at the post office.

8. Visiting people in nursing homes.

9. Taking fresh baked goods to local police and fireman.

10. Maintain a "community garden" on the grounds of your local church where the food grown can be used for benevolence in your community.

> Service opportunities take less planning and money than some of the other ideas. Small groups in the church should be challenged to make service opportunities a regular part of their focus. Imagine groups that do a weekly service project.

Also, keep in mind that…

---

[1] The **Random Acts of Kindness Institute** maintains one of the best free lists of community service ideas. Their list of ideas can be found at: http://www.randomactsofkindness.org/

> Outreach is a waste of time, effort, and money if the guests do not have a good experience when they decide to come to your church. Therefore when they come you want their experience to exceed their expectations. It is important that we remember this principle: Everything you do should be done with the first-time guest in mind. Because you never get a second chance to make a first impression. This is what we will deal with next.

Pre-service activities (From the Street to the Seat):

1. Parking:

   a. Parking spaces for first-time guests should be provided in order to ensure adequate parking.

   b. These parking spaces should be easily identifiable and accessible by the guests.

2. Entrance:

   a. Adequate signs will be available to direct people to the entrance of the church.

   b. The entrance will remain neat, uncluttered, aesthetically pleasing, and should have a nice aroma.

   c. Greeters will be at the door to greet the guests with a joyful, excited attitude and to direct people to where they need to be. Specifically greeters should:

   ➢ Be presentable in their attire and look. Make sure they are adequately supplied with breath mints and smell nice.

   ➢ Have a name tag/badge identifying them as a volunteer/team member.

   ➢ Welcome guests with a big smile and have a bulletin or service information to hand guests/attendees.

   ➢ There should be 2-3 greeters, depending on the space. You don't want to overwhelm guests with a huge army of people, but at the same time you don't want only one person hosting everyone.

   ➢ If possible, have multiple levels of greeters/hosts. If you're meeting space is a distance from the entrance, position greeters at major hallway intersections/doorways.

3. Directions:

    a. Once guests walk in the front door, besides the greeters to direct them, there should be signs pointing them in the right direction.

    b. Clarity will always ease a guest's anxiety; therefore you will need clear written signs for:

> Bathrooms.

> Kid's Areas (Elementary, Preschool, Nursery).

> Connection Areas (coffee, guest central, etc.).

> Balcony stairs.

> Class rooms.

> Staff and greeters must always be prepared and available as backup to your signs.

4. Treatment:

    a. Make every effort to cause your first-time guests to feel respected and welcome.

    b. Go above and beyond to make guests feel welcome, but do so with consistency (it is very important for both guests and regular attendees to see a consistent process in place for rolling out the 'red carpet').

    c. Have a designated hospitality area (it is good to have this space available before church, but also after in order to make sure you caught every first-time guest who came in to service).

> Staff the hospitality area with friendly, welcoming people.

> Have coffee or other drink options (tea, juice, water, etc.).

> Provide, at least during high traffic times, some kind of food option (muffins, bagels, donuts, etc.). Food can go a long way in making a solid first impression. Quality, not extravagance is the key.

> Have information about the church (Brochure, Info Cards, etc.).

5. Seating the guest:

    a. Have ushers/service hosts positioned at the back of the seating area.

    b. As guests walk into the seating area, an usher should be there as a personal guide to their seat. This usher/service host should:

        ➤ Look presentable and have some sort of name tag/badge identifying them as an official 'usher/service host.' This will help a guest understand this person was intentionally placed here to help you.

        ➤ Welcome guests with a friendly handshake and smile.

        ➤ Joyfully volunteer to help the guests find open seats.

        ➤ Ask the guests if they have a preference on the location of the seats (if space is available).

        ➤ Walk them to the best available open seat (avoid the very front row or back row).

        ➤ Kindly ask those already seated in that row to either move toward the middle or stand for the guests.

        ➤ Before the usher/service host returns to his/her post ask the guests if there is anything else he/she can do for them.

        ➤ The usher/service host then returns to his/her previous location at the back of the seating area.

> **Once a person is seated they are more prepared to enjoy the service. Remember to keep the guest in mind in all that you're doing and saying in the service. To help this first-time guest connect with the church and what it offers there has to be information gathered at some point.**

Collecting information on the guest:

1. Accomplish this during a meet-and-greet time or by passing out guest brochures before service. These brochures should have information on your church and ways to connect to the church website and church social media accounts (Facebook, Twitter,

etc.) as well as a connection card/tear-off. This connection info card contains a place for the guests to write his or her:

    a.   Name (including the name of spouse and children).

    b.   Email address.

    c.   Address and phone number.

    d.   Age bracket (include the age of children).

    e.   How they heard about the church.

    f.   Any prayer request that they may wish to share.

2. Communicate clear action steps for the card as well as give adequate time for filling it out (it can be placed in the offering at a later time).

    a.   Offer a gift to guests as an incentive for turning in the gift card in the hospitality area.

    b.   Even if the guests didn't fill one out during the service, invite every guest to the hospitality area after service. A card can be filled out there and they can be presented a gift.

    c.   Make sure the gift is something motivating (book, gift card, etc.) and not just a mug/pen with your church's logo on it.

Now that you've collected all the necessary info, you want to establish a good follow up process.

> **This step is a key one, because without follow-up, collecting the information is useless. Before actual follow-up takes place, you want to plug the information into a church database.**

Post-service follow-up:

1. Once the service is over, you need some way to connect with new guests. Every first guest is invited back to the hospitality room to meet the pastor and church staff.

a. A Guest/Information Center positioned close to the exit should also be made available for those who are in a hurry and need quick info before they leave church.

b. The info center and hospitality room should be staffed by friendly, welcoming individuals ready to meet, greet and answer any questions guests might have will provide this means.

2. Here are items that should be available at both areas:

a. Clear signage—make sure this table/area is easily accessible by guests and very clearly marked.

b. Information about the ministries offered by the church (children's, youth, small groups, etc.).

c. Information about next steps (Membership, Water Baptism, etc.).

d. Connection Cards (in case a guest has failed to get a card or loses their card).

e. A gift for first time guests—this can be either picked up at the guest's leisure or redeemed by turning in their connection card (gift suggestions: a short, but relevant book; a coffee gift card; a relevant worship CD).

f. With the gift, make sure you include a brief note/letter from your pastor thanking them for attending and inviting them back the following weekend.

Post-weekend follow-up:

1. In order to be most effective in this step of the follow-up process, make sure there is a capable staff member/volunteer taking the lead with this area.

2. Their goal is to not only follow-through with this process, but to develop a reliable team of volunteers to help, because this is usually more than one person can handle on their own.

3. Your goal with the post-weekend follow-up is to help guests see that they are valued and are a priority. In order to do this, you want to follow-up in two ways:

a. 36 Hour Email. **Note:** *This follow-up is for the guest who prefers to utilize email. If this is not the case, go to the next form of follow-up with the "Follow-up Card." (See letter d)*

    b. This email accomplishes a few things:

> Helps guests see that you appreciated them attending and then invite them back the next Sunday.

> It should be sent from the pastor (whether it actually is or not, it should be sent from him/her). This can be similar to the note/letter that is included with the free gift following the service.

> Make it as personal as possible (mention the current sermon series, and how it was great to have them in the service, etc.).

> Provide a link to a very short online survey and should seek to answer the following questions (keep it positive):

  - What did you notice first?
  - What did you like best?
  - What was your overall impression?
  - How can we pray with you?

    c. This email should be sent on Monday between 2-3 pm. This is the optimal time for someone to receive an email as it doesn't get lost in the weekend emails and is received at a time when individuals are looking for a brief distraction at work.

    d. Follow-up Card (in cases where email is not utilized by the guest). Here are a few items concerning this next step in follow-up:

> This should be sent by Tuesday at the latest. Your goal is that they receive the card by Thursday of that week.

> Make sure the greeting card/post card is packaged or printed in such a way that it stands out from all the other mail and catches the eye of the recipient.

> This is another opportunity to provide your guests with a handwritten note from the pastor in a greeting card or on the back of a postcard. (Stay away from stock letters that are impersonal).

> Make this as functional, but personal, as possible. Your goal is that guests feel noticed and valued.

> If available, include a postcard or info about your current sermon series.

One-month follow-up letter:

1. This letter is only for those guests that receive each of the previous follow-up items and yet have not returned. You don't want to be too pushy, but just let them know they are valued.

2. This letter should be sent on church letterhead from the pastor one month after their initial visit and include:

   a. Thank them for visiting last month.

   b. Explain the brief mission of your church.

   c. Touch on something that is coming up (a new series, launch of small groups, a big event, etc.).

   d. Let them know the church is available to help them in any way and they can feel free to contact the church if they need anything.

   e. Provide the necessary contact info (website would be best).

   f. Let them know you hope to see them at the church in the future.

   g. Signed by the pastor.

   h. Include an audio CD of a message that was preached over that last month.

Second-time guest follow-up:

1. Your goal in this step is very similar to your goal for first-time guests: to have them fill out the connection card, only this time check "Second-Time Guest."

   a. Your goal is not that they stay simply as guests, but that they start to take clear next steps toward discipleship/involvement.

   b. You want to give clear action steps on how to get connected (this could be printed on the guest brochure).

2. Give these "second-time guests" a chance to take a step that requires a deeper level of commitment. This is accomplished with the same Post-Service Follow-Up that the first-time guests received, but with an emphasis on connecting them with the church.

   a. 36-Hour Email—this second email should include:

   ➤ A thank you from the pastor for returning.

> ➤ An invitation to fill out a more in-depth survey:

  - ▪ What most influenced your decision to attend (Church Name) a second time?

  - ▪ What was most memorable about your first or second time at (Church Name)?

  - ▪ Would you feel comfortable inviting your friends to attend (Church Name) with you? Why?

  - ▪ How could we improve your experience?

> ➤ Based on their responses give them opportunities to take the next steps.

  b. Follow-Up Letter (again for those who do not utilize email).

> ➤ Thank them for returning.

> ➤ Invite them to let you know if there's anything the church can do to help them.

> ➤ Encourage them toward some next steps.

Gaining commitment and the new member process:

Once guests attend two times, you will want to start to connect with them. Here are a few clear steps towards making that possible.

1. New believers/Basics of Christianity small group (primarily for your un-churched new converts).

   a. This group meets for eight weeks in a relaxed discussion oriented setting.

   b. It is led by a seasoned layperson that will be able to give the new converts a strong Biblical base for why they believe what they believe and answer any questions they may have.

2. New membership classes (provided quarterly).

   a. These classes can be taught by the pastor and further intro-duce the membership candidate to the Church, its ministries, its teachings and membership requirements.

b. Each staff member will be given a chance to personally come in the class and meet the people while explaining his or her role and area of ministry within the church.

c. A discipleship evaluation form will be completed by the prospective new members to better help them find their fit in the programs available. This will include information regarding:

➢ What age group do they belong to?

➢ Do they have children who are students that are attending with them? What age group do their children belong to?

➢ How long has the individual been a Christian?

➢ Do they prefer the traditional lecture oriented teaching or a more relaxed conversational approach?

➢ Also this form will contain a list of available classes and programs with their times and dates. And the prospective member will be asked which ones they are interested in.

d. The Coordinator of Equipping Ministries[2] will meet with the class and have each person fill out a Spiritual Gift Inventory to better understand what area of ministry they are interested in.[3]

e. The prospective members, who are new to the Church of God, will be introduced to the doctrines and beliefs of the church and the required membership commitments through a series of teaching sessions (conducted by the pastor or seasoned layperson and held in no more than four hourly meetings) during the new member process.

f. Each person will fill out a membership application and sign a commitment to adhere to the requirements for membership within the Church of God (Cleveland, TN).

3. Spiritual Inventory Evaluation (this is to be accomplished after New Membership Orientation).

---

[2] Equipping is the ministries of helping individuals grow in their relationship with Jesus, by providing innovative and effective resources for identifying, equipping, and releasing people into their gift-based ministries. Having a qualified candidate who can coordinate this ministry is an invaluable asset.

[3] A booklet on spiritual gifts inventory can be purchased from www.churchgrowth.org also on this site a free spiritual gifts analysis is available. Other online sources also offer free spiritual gift invitatory/analysis.

      a. This will be a scheduled meeting with the coordinator of Equipping Ministries, in which the results of the person's Spiritual Gift Inventory will be shared on an individual basis.

      b. At this point the coordinator of Equipping Ministry will seek to connect the person with an area of ministry that fits their gifting and interests.

> **Have clear scheduled times for important events in this process. Clarity helps to create movement through your assimilation and discipleship planning.**

Finding a place—the process of ongoing involvement:

Once a person becomes a member they are assigned an Elder[4] who will provide care and follow up. Besides managing care (special needs, hospital visits, etc.) the Elders should adhere to these guidelines on future follow-ups when they find their people missing from church.

1. Absent for three successive weeks:

    a. Send a "We've Missed You" post card.

    b. Include a brief handwritten note on the back of the postcard expressing that you have missed having them at a service. **Note:** This can be subjective. If you see a person's name on the three-week absent list that was away for a valid reason, use discretion in sending them a card.

2. Absent for four successive weeks:

    a. The elder will need to follow-up with a phone call.

    b. The goal of this call is to not condemn them for not attending, but just to make sure everything is okay.

3. Absent for eight successive weeks:

    a. Send a letter from the pastor expressing the "we have missed you" message as well as the elder making another phone call.

---

[4] Each elder has the duty of serving as shepherds under the shepherd. Meaning that under the leadership of the senior pastor they help to give pastoral care to the members of their assigned group. This ministry becomes more valuable as the church grows and the senior pastor's responsibilities increase. (See Section 14 on Ministry of Elders).

    b. Include a short description of an event that is coming up at the church and invite them to it.

   4. Absent eight plus successive weeks:

    a. Keep them on an 'outreach' mailing list, but discontinue follow-up with them unless they connect again with the church.

    b. The elder will continue to be the key person to keep tabs on the attendance patterns of your people.

The coordinator of Equipping Ministries will be responsible for keeping the people connected to ministry opportunities within the church.

   1. New members will be mentored in a process toward becoming ministers to others, as they use their gifts to serve their Lord.

    a. After the initial placement in a ministry role, new members will work closely to the ministry team leader of their particular area.

    b. Although each department will have a monthly meeting, individuals will have a weekly opportunity to give feedback on how they feel this new ministry role is working with them as they serve alongside the team leader.

    c. The new member will undergo a re-evaluation of their ministry involvement, as the coordinator of Equipping Ministry will meet with the ministry leaders at this time to discuss the process and progress of each person.

   2. New members will be encouraged along the way.

    a. They will receive a personalized-monthly newsletter or email from the Coordinator of Equipping Ministries commending them for their work and efforts.

    b. To recognize the efforts of Men's Discipleship and their workers a banquet will be held once a year.

    c. The workers assimilated into the program will receive a letter with a personalized message once a year from the pastor to evaluate the current emotional and spiritual contentment regarding the area where they are serving. This letter will act as a feedback form that the member can return to the church office.

Each new attendee will be encouraged to "plug in" to an area of Christian Discipleship.

1. Options for the new families will have been made clear early in the assimilation process, and an interest evaluation form will have been completed.

2. Once an interest has been shown, discipleship leaders are encouraged to actively seek the involvement of the new members into their programs.

> **The continued involvement of a new member in the church will depend upon the level of satisfaction they discover by what they are able to contribute as well as the quality of ministry that they are receiving.**

A final note TO ALL PASTORS, CHURCH STAFF, AND LAY LEADERS:

All of the concepts in this document are intended to be launching points for the assimilation ministry of your local church. It would be virtually impossible to duplicate every single facet of this process at once. Begin with small changes, implementing ideas a few at a time. Get creative with original ideas of your own. Think about what would work well in your church as well as what would not. Your ultimate goal is to facilitate the necessary changes in your current plan that will produce lasting results. The important thing to remember is to make the effort, because having a quality assimilation plan in place will help to close the back door of your church so that the God-given potential of ministry in your local community can be reached. God bless you in your efforts!

SECTION 14

Elders Manual

Ministry of Elders

Statement of Purpose

The elders of the church *provide care* for the people and serve as *shepherds to the flock of God*. This is the mandate given to elders in 1 Peter 5:1-10. As shepherds who work under the supervision and authority of the pastor, each elder must seek *first* to be a caregiver to the people of God's church.

S   The elder is a public SERVANT.

H   The elder is a HELPER to the pastor.

E   The elder is an EXHORTER and EDIFIER of the people.

P   The elder is a PRAYER PARTNER to the pastor and each member of his oversight.

H   The elder is a model of genuine HUMILITY.

E   The elder is an EVANGELIST who leads people to the Lord.

R   The elder is a spiritual ROLE MODEL to the people he serves.

D   The elder is one who DISCIPLES new converts and growing Christians.

The Office of Elder

In the Old Testament the office of elder was established for the oversight of the community of faith. In the New Testament, the office is continued and developed. There are two names used interchangeably in the New Testament to refer to the office of elder. These names are "elder" (Titus 1:5), and "shepherd" or "overseer" (1 Timothy 3:1).

The words *elder* and *shepherd* are used in conjunction with one another. In 1 Peter 5:1, 2, for instance, Peter addresses the elders among his listeners and tells them to shepherd God's flock. Another passage describing the interchangeability of these terms is Acts 20. Paul is speaking to the *elders* of the church at Ephesus (v.17). He tells them to keep watch over themselves and all the flock of which the Holy Spirit had made them overseers (v.28) and to shepherd the church of God.

The word *elder* comes from the Greek transliterated word *presbuteuros,* which, in regard to the office of an elder, speaks of the dignity and honor of those who exercise leadership in the church. The word is of Hebrew origin and background where, in Jewish life, it referred to age and then to the position of leadership held by the Sanhedrin. The early church borrowed the idea of elder leadership from the synagogue pattern and incorporated it into their government structure. The world *elder* then, in the New Testament, speaks not primarily of age, but of the dignity, honor, and maturity of the office holder and the necessary quality of life that must be present in the person who would hold that office.

Those who would fill this office for overseeing in their local church are called elders. Selected by the pastor, the elders are to watch over the spiritual welfare of the church family. Where appropriate, they are to watch over the spiritual welfare of that portion of the church committed to them. The elders come along side the pastor to assist him in caring for the welfare of the whole of the church.

The Life of Elder

According to Scripture, those who bear this office would exhibit certain characteristics of life. This includes being blameless in life, sound in the faith, wise in the things of God, and discreet in all things. Persons who fill this office should exhibit a lifestyle that is an example to all, both inside and outside the church. A congregation preparing to affirm persons to this holy office should carefully study appropriate passages of scripture relating to the elder and be very prayerful in affirming persons to this office.

Scripture gives us two basic passages that describe the qualifications for elders: 1 Timothy 3:1-7 and Titus 1:6-9.

1. Elders must be dedicated Christians whose outward lives bear witness to the transforming power of the grace of God.

2. They must be men and women of integrity in all personal relationships, both in and out of the church.

3. They must be honest.

4. They must be above reproach; blameless, presenting no patterns of scriptural disobedience or grounds for accusation.

5. They must have a reputation for godliness wherever they are known.

6. They must be exemplary in their "churchmanship." Except for unavoidable work conflicts, family vacations, and health problems, we expect our elders to attend all the services of the church. People who look to elders have a right to see them present, hear them pray, see them minister, and see them manifesting spiritual life and interest.

7. Elders must set a good example for the other members in the stewardship of their money. Elders must be "storehouse tithers." They should also participate in other offerings such as faith promises, debt reductions, and special offerings. No person shall allow himself/herself to be considered for the office of elder who does not tithe.

(Tithing is the giving of 10 percent of one's income into the treasury of their local church.)

8.   Elders are expected to attend the scheduled meetings for their offices. All persons permitting themselves to serve as elders are stating that they are committed to attending regularly scheduled meetings, as well as specially called meetings. Recurring non-attendance is cause for removal from office.

9.   They ought to believe in the church, to love her even as Christ did, and to seek to increase her usefulness and effectiveness in the cause for reaching people for Christ.

10.   Elders must be temperate: sober, free from excesses.

11.   They must be self-controlled: not impulsive, but able to temper desires, impulses, and appetites; God-controlled.

12.   They must be respectable, leading an orderly and honorable life.

13.   Elders must be hospitable: friendly, sharing resources with others.

14.   They must be able to teach; accurately explain God's Word so as to instruct others in the faith and refute those who contradict the truth.

15.   They must not be given to alcoholic beverages, no indulgence in mind-altering chemicals (legal or not), and must be free from addictions (including, but not limited to, tobacco, and marijuana).

16.   Elders must not be violent, but gentle: not a quick temper, not abusive of others, but of a kind and considerate spirit.

17.   They must not be quarrelsome: not prone toward selfish arguments; but one who pursues understanding, agreement and common interests.

18.   Elders must not be a lover of money: not motivated by money; must not be stingy, but rather an example in giving.

19.   They must be the husband of one wife. They must be devoted to the integrity, purity, chastity and stability of the home, especially the marriage and husband/wife relationship, a covenant keeper at home, and absolutely opposed to polygamy.

20.   Elders manage their family well; a well-ordered household; a healthy family life and well-behaved children; a parent faithful to the parenting process.

21. Elders are not new believers: they must have been a Christian long enough to demonstrate the reality of their conversion, the depth of their spirituality, and the promise of God's destiny for their ministry of servant leadership.

22. They must not be overbearing: must not be stubborn, insensitive or prone to force opinions on others; must be more interested in service than self-pleasure; must be willing to listen to and respect others; must be willing to prefer others before self.

23. Elders are not quick-tempered: must be able to exercise self-control and patience in difficult situations; always gentle and redemptive in relational struggles.

24. They love what is good: must desire the will of God in every decision; pray, hope, and work for the best/highest good to be realized.

25. Elders do not pursue dishonest gain: are upright in their business dealings.

26. Elders must be fair and impartial. Judgments must be based on scriptural principles.

27. Elders must be holy, reverent, continually desiring to be separated from sin: must be devoted to prayer, the study of Scripture and the guarding of their own spiritual walk; must be committed to the process of wholeness and soundness of life which comes through an ongoing journey with God from the new birth to heaven.

28. They must hold firmly to the trustworthy message; must be stable in the faith, obedient to the Word of God, continually seeking to be controlled by the Holy Spirit.

29. Elders must be sexually pure: not involved in adultery, fornication, homosexuality, sexually suggestive behavior, pornography, or sexual addiction. They must be morally upright. Behavior with the opposite gender, same gender, or toward oneself, must be proper and becoming, holy and righteous.

30. They must be full of the Holy Spirit and wisdom (see Acts 6:3).

31. Elders must agree with and live by the doctrine (as set forth in the Declaration of Faith) and polity of the local church, and the by-laws of the General Assembly of the Church of God (Cleveland, TN).

The Responsibilities of an Elder

1. To be in a personal, dynamic, growing relationship with the Lord. Elders are to be an example to the family of God. They are to provide a scriptural role model and are to set a pattern before the family of God of a rightly ordered life, with a single purpose: to glorify God (see 1 Peter 5:3).

2. To pursue agreement with and promote the mission given by God to the local church.

3. To monitor and facilitate the spiritual life of the church and the development of its members. Serving in all humility, elders are to assist the pastor in guiding, directing, guarding, and protecting the members of the body; seeking to meet their spiritual needs and assisting in warning against harmful influences and guarding against false teachers (see Acts 20:28; 1 Peter 5:3).

4. Elders are to serve in a spirit of love, humility, and submission as servants of the Most High. They admonish, refute, and confront those who contradict the Word of God, and who are teaching what they should not be teaching or who are continuing in a pattern of behavior contradictory to biblical truth. Elders are to close potential entrances for Satan so that the truth of Christ will remain credible to both the congregation and the community (see Acts 20:29-3; Titus 1:9).

5. Elders are to participate in the ministry of worship and service to seek to lead people into a personal relationship with Jesus Christ as Savior and Lord.

6. Elders help ensure that the church is following the leadership of Jesus Christ, our Head (see 1 Timothy 3:4, 5; 5:17; Hebrews 13:17).

7. Elders are to encourage the family of God at their local church. They are to make it a priority to pray and know God's Word and will so they may work in harmony with the pastor to communicate the vision and purpose of their church. Thus, they would be equipped to help instruct the church in what God desires and encourage them with sound teaching (see Acts 6:1-4; 1 Timothy 3:22; Titus 1:9).

8. Elders are to help provide for ministries in accord with the Holy Spirit and the mission of the local church.

9. Elders are to work with the pastor in establishing purposes and goals according to God-given direction.

10. Elders, along with the pastor, welcome members into the local church family.

11. Elders give oversight to the ministries of the church under the direction of the pastor.

12. Elders facilitate flexible organizational structures that will advance the ministries of the church and her God-given mission, recognizing that the church is an organism.

13. Elders give direct spiritual support to those members of the Body who have been assigned to them for encouragement, teaching, prayer, visitation, and spiritual nurture.

14. Elders promote worship, spiritual growth and development, care, and nurture; they share the good news; they help advance the kingdom of God and the growth and grace and truth in all.

15. Elders are to be intimately involved in ministry.

16. Elders are to be an example to the local church body in regular attendance, prayer, spirituality, tithing (tithing is the paying of 10 percent of one's gross income into the local church treasury), giving, attitude, righteousness, and servanthood. Their very being will turn others to Christ, rather than away.

17. Elders will meet with the pastor monthly.

18. All of the elders will lay hands upon the pastor and pray before each service.

19. Elders and their spouses will serve as an Altar Team. They will also pray with congregants at other times as called upon.

20. Elders will visit the elderly, the home bound, those hospitalized or in nursing homes.

21. Elders will serve as the spiritual caretaker with an oversight of a proportion of the congregation.

22. Elders may serve as an advisor to the pastor in spiritual matters.

23. Elders may assist in serving Communion.

24. Elders will anoint the sick with oil and pray for them.

25. Elders will serve the local church in disciplinary matters when called upon by the pastor.

26. When the pastor is unavailable for service (when he would serve if available), an elder will represent the church in his absence.

Principle Objective: Elders will help create and monitor an atmosphere of healing, care, nurture, and spiritual growth within the local church body.

Selection of Elders

Scripture gives evidence of the first elders being appointed by the founders of the church. By this example, it is implied that the existing spiritual leadership of a church be intimately involved in the process of selecting elders to ensure selection based on spiritual character, rather than personal preference or popular opinion. Beyond this, there are no specific scriptural guidelines given regarding the selection process (see Acts 14:23; Titus 1:5).

1. The pastor of the local church, having sought the Lord in prayer and being led by the Holy Spirit, will choose those men who meet the qualifications for elders as given in Scripture. The pastor will then contact those persons, giving each prospect a copy of the qualifications and responsibilities for serving as an elder, along with a written response form for accepting or declining the proposal for serving as an elder.

2. Persons who have been contacted about becoming elders will then engage in prayer, self-appraisal, and personal evaluation in light of Scriptural qualification. Any prospective elder may withdraw their name at this point if they do not set their heart on being an elder or if they do not meet the qualifications. Those persons who agree to serve as an elder will then return the written form to the pastor indicating whether they accept or decline the opportunity to serve as an elder. Persons who do not return the written form to the pastor will be regarded as having withdrawn from the elder process.

3. The pastor will meet personally and privately with each prospective elder to discuss the office and their qualifications. Following this meeting with the pastor, after prayerful consideration by both the pastor and the prospective elder, and following thorough examination by both in regard to the biblical qualifications of the office, the prospective elder's name will be presented to the local church congregation and be "set forth" for ministry as an elder.

Terms of Elders

1. Scripture does not establish length of tenure for serving as an elder. Instead, from Scripture the implication is that an elder serves for as long as he is qualified and is willing to serve.

2. Each year the elder will be subject to review, recommitment and reaffirmation and shall be presented to the congregation for rededication.

3. During the period of annual review, both the individual and other elders shall evaluate their continued service as elders, again considering the biblical qualifications, as well as any personal factors that might effect their service. An individual's service as an elder may be discontinued by his own decision or by the pastor.

4. Those elders renewing their commitment would again be presented to the congregation of the church for affirmation and dedication. A person's leaving the board of elders would not preclude his service as a future elder, subject to the regular elder selection process.

5. Other elders may be added to the elder board by the pastor and would go through the regular selection process.

How Elders Relate

Introduction: To function as an effective ministry team, elders must maintain harmonious relationships with their pastoral leaders and with other elders. The Bible offers clear instruction on how they are to relate to one other.

1. Mutual Submission

Submit to one another out of reverence for Christ (Ephesians 5:21).

2. Mutual Respect

For by the grace given me I say to everyone of you: Do not think of yourself more highly than you ought, but rather think of yourself with sober judgment, in accordance with the measure of faith God has given you . . . Live in harmony with one another. Do not be proud, but be willing to associate with people of low position. Do not be conceited (Romans 12:3,16).

3. Christian Love

If I speak in the tongues of men and of angels, but have not love, I am only a resounding gong or a clanging cymbal. If I have the gift of prophecy and can fathom all mysteries and all knowledge, and if I have a faith that can move mountains, but have not love, I am nothing. If I give all I possess to the poor and surrender my body to the flames, but have not love, I gain nothing. Love is patient, love is kind. It does not envy, it does not boast, it is not proud. It is not rude, it is not self-seeking, it is not easily angered, it keeps no record of wrongs. Love does not delight in evil but rejoices with the truth. It always protects, always trusts, always hopes, always perseveres. Love never fails. But where there are prophecies, they will cease: where there are tongues, they will be stilled: where there is knowledge, it will pass away. For we know in part and we prophesy in part, but when perfection comes, the imperfect disappears. When I was a child, I talked like a child, I thought like a child, I reasoned like a child. When I became a man, I put childish ways behind me. Now we see but a poor reflection as in a mirror: then we shall see face to face. Now I know in part: then I shall know fully, even as I am fully known. And now these three remain: faith, hope and love. But the greatest of these is love (1 Corinthians 13:1-13).

4. **Brotherhood**

Be devoted to one another in brotherly love. Honor one another above yourselves (Romans 12:10).

How to Be a Pastor-Extender

Scripture Text: Exodus 18:13-26

Introduction: How can an elder be an extension of the pastor's ministry?

1. Pray for the pastor and his family (Philippians 1:19, 20).

2. Provide a hedge of protection around the pastor and his family (Job 1:10).

3. Hold up the pastor's hands in battle (Exodus 17:8-16). How?

   A. Spirituality: "*Choose some of our men*" (verse 9).

   B. Vulnerability: "*Aaron and Hur went*" (verse 10)

   C. Responsibility: "*Held up his hands*" (verse 11)

   D. Mutuality: "*Took a stone ... held his hands*" (verse 12)

   E. Adaptability: "*Remained steady till sunset*" (verse 12)

   F. Potentiality: "*Joshua overcame the Amalekite army*" (verse 13)

4. Exhibit unity (Psalm 133:1; Ephesians 4:3; Acts 1:4; 2:1)

5. Show up (Hebrews 10:25)

6. Know the pastor (1 Thessalonians 5:11-13). Five Assumptions:

   A. He doesn't have to be perfect to be valuable–he is not perfect.

   B. He doesn't have to please everybody–he can't please everybody.

   C. You don't bear personal responsibility for his behavior–he is responsible for his own behavior.

   D. Diversion is necessary–he needs time away from "ministry" to replenish his energy and vision.

7. Understand the pastor's various roles and responsibilities:

    A.   He is a father.

    B.   He is a pastor/teacher.

    C.   He is an administrator.

    D.   He is a representative of the local church family and the denomination.

8. Be patient with the pastor as he learns to delegate tasks and authority to the elders (Philippians 3:12; Titus 2:2).

9. Be assertive in ministering to the needs of the congregation. Elders are under-shepherds of the *flock of God* (1 Peter 5:1-4; Romans 12:11).

10. Be willing to share respectfully and privately with the pastor if the Holy Spirit reveals to you blind spots regarding his leadership (Galatians 1:8,9; 1 Corinthians 4:14,21; 1 Timothy 5:1; 2 Timothy 4:2).

11. Do the work of an evangelist (2 Timothy 4:5).

12. Love one another (1 John 3:14,16).

13. Know the great shepherdly principle: a flock cannot be driven; it must be led (Genesis 33:13,14).

The material presented can be adapted to fit the needs of the local congregation.

The following resources were used in compiling this *Elders Manual*:

Elder Ministry Resource Manual by Raymond Culpepper;

Elders' Manual by Bryan Cutshall;

Elders Manual by French Arrington;

Elders Manual by Larry L. Benz.

SECTION 15
LifeBuilders
FORMS

LifeBuilders forms are available at
www.coglifebuilders.com

LifeBuilders Charter Application or Update

Choose one: Charter Application ☐   Change in Pastor/Team Leadership ☐

Pastor Contact Information

Name	Church
Church Address	Church File No.
City	State Zip
Church Phone	Cell Phone
Email	

LifeBuilders Leader Contact Information

Name	☐ Leader
Home Address	
City	State Zip
Day Phone	Cell Phone
Email	

LifeBuilders Team Members Contact Information

Name	☐ Leadership Team ☐ Member
Home Address	
City	State Zip
Day Phone	Cell Phone
Email	Position:

LifeBuilders Men's Discipleship Team (continued)
Contact Information

Name	☐ Leadership Team ☐ Member
Home Address	
City	State Zip
Day Phone	Cell Phone
Email	Position:

Name	☐ Leadership Team ☐ Member:
Home Address	
City	State Zip
Day Phone	Cell Phone
Email	Position:

Name	☐ Leadership Team ☐ Member
Home Address	
City	State Zip
Day Phone	Cell Phone
Email	Position:

Please make additional copies of this form as needed.

Four ways to update:

Online: www.coglifebuilders.com

Fax: 423-478-7288

Mail: Church of God Men's Discipleship; PO Box 2430, Cleveland, TN 37320

E-mail: mensdiscipleship@churchofgod.org

LifeBuilders Annual Report Form

Report Date November 30, _____ (year)

LifeBuilders Leader Name _____

☐ Please check if your LifeBuilders leadership team has changed since your last report (please submit your changes on the contact info form above).

Report submitted by _____

Pastor's Name _____

Church File No. _____

Church Name _____

Address _____

City _____

State _____   Zip _____

ATTENDANCE

Number of men in LifeBuilders this report period _____

Number of meetings this report period _____

Number of prayer meetings _____

Number of Bible studies _____

Special meetings:

    Theme _____

    Topic _____

    Subjects covered _____

Men on Mission _____

LIFEBUILDERS DISCIPLESHIP INITIATIVE
Transformation Small Groups

Number of small groups _____

Number of men participating _____

Book Studies

Book completed _____

Number of men _____

Book completed _____

Number of men _____

Book completed _____

Number of men _____

PASTOR'S PRAYER PARTNERS PROGRAM

Do you have a Pastor's Prayer Partners Program?   ☐ Yes ☐ No

If yes, number of men participating _____

If no, (1) Do you plan to organize soon?   ☐ Yes ☐ No

       (2) Would you like more information?   ☐ Yes ☐ No

MEN'S DISCIPLESHIP E-CONNECT

Please send us testimonies, pictures, etc., from your LifeBuilders group.
We will place these in our Men's Discipleship E-connect emailed periodically to all LifeBuilders men.

PASTOR APPRECIATION

Did you sponsor a Pastors Appreciation Day?   ☐ Yes ☐ No

LIFEBUILDERS IDEA CALENDAR OF ACTIVITIES FOR ONE YEAR

This is only a guide to show the available programs and when they can be planned. Insert other programs and activities as needed.

	JANUARY	FEBRUARY	MARCH
WINTER	• Arrange a planning session for year's activities • Plan men on mission teams • Network with Men of Action and attend annual rally • Begin planning your Pastor's Prayer Partner Program • Promote individual "Read through the Bible"campaign READ	• Host a Valentine Sweetheart Banquet • Organize a lay retreat • Organize prayer meetings • Plan & start a transformational group Bible study • Begin planning a Resurrection Breakfast	• Oraganize the Pastor's Prayer Partner Program • Plan and Promote Devoted Family Discipleship emphasis • Partner with boys ministry to reach & disciple boys.
	APRIL	**MAY**	**JUNE**
SPRING	• Observe Pastor Appreciation Day • Sponsor a Resurrection Breakfast • Plan fund-raising projects • Host a bosses and coworkers dinner	• Give a special recognition on Mother's Day • Sponsor a fund-raising project • Have a family picnic • Plan a fishing tournament and cookout • Participate in Devoted Family Discipleship Program	• Promote Father's Day Observance • Have a father/son outing • Sponsor a chili cook-off
	JULY	**AUGUST**	**SEPTEMBER**
SUMMER	• Have a father/son overnight camp-out • Men on a mission project • Hold a "Freedom Celebration Breakfast" (celebrate July 4)	• Set up outreach ministries (fall emphasis) • Conduct a "Men's Prayer Seminar" • Sponsor a golf or fishing tournament • Begin another small group Bible study	• Oganize a tract distributrion program • Sponsor a fund-raising project • Have a father/daughter banquet or outing • Conduct a "Christian Manhood Video Training" seminar
	OCTOBER	**NOVEMBER**	**DECEMBER**
FALL	• Observe LifeBuilders Recognition Day • Participate in Men's Ministries Enlistment Week • Observe National Clergy Appreciation (if not observed in April) • Elect Men's Ministries officers	• Mail yearly Men's Mnistries report to Life-Builders national office • Help the needy • Sponsor Thanksgiving outreach services in nursing gomes, jails, prisons, etc. • Deliver Thanksgiving food baskets	• Participate in family outreach to the needy (food, gifts, clothing) • Sponsor a couples Christmas dinner • Plan and sponsor a watchnight service • Promote READ Program • Thank God for a successful year!

LIFEBUILDERS
PROGRAM PLANNING GUIDE

TYPE OF MEETING:

☐breakfast ☐cookout ☐luncheon ☐banquet ☐other

Date of meeting _____ Meeting Place _____

Meal starting time _____ Cost of meal _____

Coordinator of meal function _____ Phone _____

Chairman of Meeting _____ Music coordinator

Song leader _____ Special singers _____

Musicians _____

Speaker for meeting _____

Theme for meeting _____

Purpose of meeting _____

Scripture and prayer _____

Planning and preparation before meeting _____

Plans and announcements for future meetings _____

Minutes of previous meeting _____

Publicity _____

Offering _____

Materials and equipment needed _____

Other men who will participate _____

Testimonies _____

Closing the meeting _____

Use this form for making plans for your regular men's meeting. This form may be duplicated.

CONFIDENTIAL

LifeBuilders
Pastor's Endorsement Form

Men's Leader Information

Men's Leader: Please complete this section, then give this form to your pastor.

Name _____ Social Security Number _____

Address _____

_____

Home Phone Number _____ Cell Phone Number _____

Email _____

Date of Birth _____ Married ☐ Single ☐

Local Church _____

Pastor's Information

Pastor: Please complete this section then mail this form to your administrative bishop.

Pastor's Name _____

Name of Local Church _____

Address _____

_____

Church Phone Number _____

I certify that the LifeBuilders men's leader mentioned above meets the following requirements for certification as a LifeBuilders Men's Leader.

1. Be a loyal member of the Church of God, adhering to its teachings.
2. Be baptized in the Holy Spirit.
3. Be faithful in tithing.
4. Be a regular church attendant.
5. Be one who works in harmony with the local, state, and international church's program and one who reflects a cooperative attitude toward the progress of the church.
6. Be endorsed by the senior pastor.
7. Background check has been conducted on the men's leader above.

Pastor's Signature _____

LifeBuilders Checkup

(This form is to help determine the progress of your LifeBuilders Ministry and identify specific actions for improvement and growth).

1. Do you have the support of your pastor?

2. Do you have a clear mission and vision?

3. Has the LifeBuilders leader received Level 2 Leadership Training?

4. Has your LifeBuilders team been selected?

5. Has the LifeBuilders Leadership Team received at least Level 1 Training?

6. Are LifeBuilders Leadership Team members involved in a Transformational Small Group?

7. Have you had your kickoff meeting?

8. Is your LifeBuilders ministry chartered?

9. Have you selected and trained your small group leaders?

10. Do you have monthly LifeBuilders meetings?

11. Have you launched Transformational Small Groups?

12. Does your Pastor's Prayer Partner Ministry function consistently?

13. Do you communicate well? (Email, brochures, website, text messages, newsletters, or other ways?)

14. Have special days or big events to provide entry points for men into LifeBuilders ministry?

15. What percentage of the men of your church are involved in Transformational Small Groups?

16. Do you celebrate your victories?

SECTION 16

LifeBuilders Certification Kit

LifeBuilders Certification Kit $60.00 (Regular cost – $93.95)

- *LifeBuilders Leadership Certification Manual* - $25
- *LifeBuilders Essentials* - $20
- *LifeBuilders Essentials Leadership* CD - $15
- *James, A Path to Discipleship* - $16.95
- *Praying the Breath of Life* – $15.95

SECTION 17

LifeBuilders Leadership Certification Manual Review

REVIEW

Section 1

1. What are the benefits of LifeBuilders Discipleship Ministry for the men?

2. What are the benefits of LifeBuilders Discipleship Ministry for the pastor?

3. What are the requirements for LifeBuilders Leadership Certification Level 1?

4. What are the requirements for LifeBuilders Leadership Certification Level 2?

5. Who can teach Level 1 Certification classes?

Section 2

6. Identify 12 keys to starting a LifeBuilders Discipleship Ministry?

Section 3

7. What five areas should we evaluate to determine if our church welcomes men?

9. What are the pastor's responsibilities for LifeBuilders ministry?

10. What is the vision of LifeBuilders Discipleship Ministry?

11. List nine characteristics LifeBuilders Leaders must have.

12. Name three parts of a testimony.

13. What are the three basic types of leaders?

14. Name three pointers for the first meeting.

15. Content for your meeting should include the following:

16.   What are the responsibilities for Leadership Team Members?

17.   Name five elements of a kickoff meeting.

18.   What five elements are essential when training the LifeBuilders Leadership Team?

19.   Why are small groups important?

20.   Name six keys to keeping men active.

21.   What training/ministry opportunities are available through the Church of God?

22.   What are the objectives of the Family Discipleship Initiative?

23.   Name six LifeBuilders Ministries that bring change and support discipleship for men and families.

24.   What is required for men to receive the LifeBuilders Discipleship100 Certificate and be recognized as a commissioned man?

25. What is required for men to receive the LifeBuilders Discipleship 200 Certificate?

26. Name six opportunities for ministry training and Involvement

27. What is step one to connecting with new men?

28. Name five natural ministry times to build relationships with men and get them into LifeBuilders Discipleship Ministry.

29. How many momentum-building events should be planned annually?

Review with Answers

LifeBuilders Leadership Certification Manual
Review With Answers

Section 1

1. What are the benefits of LifeBuilders Discipleship Ministry for the men?

- Disciples men.

- Equips and trains men for ministry.

- Mobilizes men for work in the church.

- Enables men to experience spiritual renewal.

- Provides men encouragement, accountability and a sense of belonging.

- Encourages men to be better husbands, fathers, providers and spiritual leaders.

- Provides a central purpose of mission.

- Organizes prayer support for the pastor and vital ministries of the church.

2. What are the benefits of LifeBuilders Discipleship Ministry for the pastor?

- Provides support for the pastor.

- Provides able and wise leadership to help the pastor.

- Develops men to do the work of ministry.

- Provides prayer support through the Pastor's Prayer Partners program.

3. What are the requirements for LifeBuilders Leadership Certification Level 1?

    (1)   Attend a LifeBuilders Leadership Certification Class led by LifeBuilders Leader with Level 2 Certification.

    (2)   Complete the review at the end of the manual.

    (3)   Have pastor's confidential endorsement.

    (4)   Have a completed background check.

    (5)   Participation in a chartered LifeBuilders Ministry

4. What are the requirements for LifeBuilders Leadership Certification Level 2?

You must attend a LifeBuilders Leadership Certification Conference and meet the following criteria.

    (1)   Complete the review at the end of the Certification Manual.

    (2)   Have pastor's confidential endorsement.

    (3)   Have a completed background.

    (4)   Charter and Leadership Team Forms must be up-to-date at the Men's Discipleship International Office.

5. Who can teach Level 1 Certification classes?

Men who have attended a LifeBuilders Leadership Certification Conference and are certified at Level 2

Section 2

6. Identify 12 keys to starting a LifeBuilders Discipleship Ministry?

    (1)   The pastor.

    (2)   Have a clear mission and vision.

    (3)   Strong LifeBuilders Leader.

(4)   Build the LifeBuilders Team.

(5)   Train the LifeBuilders Leadership Team.

(6)   Schedule a Leadership Team Kickoff Meeting.

(7)   Charter your local LifeBuilders Discipleship Ministry.

(8)   Select and train small group leaders.

(9)   Plan a big event to create momentum for LifeBuilders ministry.

(10) Start monthly LifeBuilders meetings.

(11) Launch Transformational Small Groups.

(12) Pastor's Prayer Partners.

Section 3

7. What five areas should we evaluate to determine if our church welcomes men?

(1) Appearance and décor of the church

(2) Dress of the congregation

(3) Music

(4) Preaching and teaching

(5) Value of the church toward men

8. What is the portal priority or central mission of LifeBuilders?

Discipleship

9. What are the pastor's responsibilities for LifeBuilders ministry?

- Initiate the selection of team leaders and discipleship team

- Oversee discipleship process of the LifeBuilders Leader and Leadership Team

- Provide guidance

- Encourage participation

- Organize a Prayer Partners Team

- Sponsor activities for men

10. What is the vision of LifeBuilders Discipleship Ministry?

Every man a disciple

11. List nine characteristics LifeBuilders leaders must have.

(1) LifeBuilders leaders must be able to share their testimony.

(2) LifeBuilders leaders must be disciples.

(3) LifeBuilders leaders must be men of the Word.

(4) LifeBuilders leaders must be men of prayer.

(5) LifeBuilders leaders must be led by the Holy Spirit.

(6) LifeBuilders leaders must be worshippers.

(7) LifeBuilders leaders must be faithful to God.

(8) LifeBuilders leaders must be passionate about reaching and discipling men.

(9) LifeBuilders leaders must allow God to develop their leadership gifts.

12. Name three parts of a testimony.

(1) What you were like before you came to Christ

(2) How you came to Christ

(3) What difference has coming to Christ meant in your life and family.

13. What are the three basic types of leaders?

(1) Those who are now involved

(2) Those who are in training to become leaders

(3) Those who feel that God is calling them in this area

14. Name three pointers for the first meeting.

(1) Keep the first meeting to a maximum of one hour.

(2) Share your vision for the men of the church. To reach and win men to Christ and to disciple them into an authentic Christ-centered relationship.

(3) Answer key questions before the meeting:

  a. What is the main goal?

  b. Why do we want a men's ministry in the church?

  c. What methods will we use—what is our philosophy of ministry?

  d. How will we create, capture, and sustain momentum among our men?

  e. Do we have ideas about what activities and programs we might incorporate into our ministry?

  f. How can we demonstrate that a healthy men's ministry will strengthen the whole church?

15. Content for your meeting should include the following:

(1) Begin with prayer (about five minutes).

(2) Review the history of ministry to men in your church (about five minutes).

(3) Be up front and honest about the blessing and the burdens of previous attempts at men's ministry.

(4) Share the potential of a new or renewed LifeBuilders men's discipleship.

(5) Talk a little about the present environment for reaching men (about 15 minutes).

       a. How are men doing?

       b. What are their problems?

       c. How should the church respond?

(6) Review the potential of discipling and training the men of your church.

(7) Closing comments:

> "It seems clear that God is calling us to reach the men of our church and help them grow. I would like to suggest that, together, we go through a three-week process of designing a men's ministry for our church using the Church of God LifeBuilders men's discipleship material as a guide. Who would like to give it a try?"

16. What are the responsibilities for Leadership Team Members?

(1) Strategy and coordination

(2) Community

(3) Prayer and intercession

(4) Team leader

(5) Ministry projects and resources

(6) New positions. Add new positions to the leadership team.

17. Name five elements of a kickoff meeting.

(1) Cast the vision

(2) State the purpose

(3) Connect LifeBuilders to the church vision

(4) Show the positive benefits of this effort

(5) Explain the commitment

18. **What five elements are essential when training the LifeBuilders Leadership Team?**

    (1) Small Groups

    (2) Prayer

    (3) Certification Manual

    (4) LifeBuilders Essentials

    (5) Commitment

19. **Why are small groups important?**

    (1) Follows the model of Jesus

    (2) Builds relationships

    (3) Builds in accountability

    (4) Discipleship is best facilitated in small groups.

    (5) Each man helps others grow.

    (6) Partnership for growing in Christ and for ministry

    (7) It is scriptural

20. **Name six keys to keeping men active.**

    (1) Consistent LifeBuilders meetings

    (2) Relationships

    (3) Help men discover their purpose

    (4) Get men involved in the life and ministry of the church

    (5) On mission with Christ

    (6) Needs met

21. What training/ministry opportunities are available through the Church of God?

- LifeBuilders Men of Legacy Conference

- LifeBuilders Roundtables

- LifeBuilders Leadership Certification Conference

- LifeBuilders Leadership Training Conference

- LifeBuilders Rallies

- Marriage & Family Conference/Retreat

- Elders Training

22. What are the objectives of the Family Discipleship Initiative?

(1) Help families develop the habit of family worship/discipleship time together

(2) Help families make family discipleship a lifestyle

(3) Support family revival and healing

(4) Challenge every family member to be a disciple of Jesus Christ making disciples

(5) Raise up godly men and women who will raise their families with the commitment, "As for me and my house, we will serve the Lord."

(6) Provide an opportunity for fathers, mothers, and heads of households to have a fresh beginning as spiritual leaders

(7) To support foundational theological beliefs

23. Name six LifeBuilders Ministries that bring change and support discipleship for men and families.

(1) Transformational Small Groups/Bible Studies

(2) Family Discipleship Initiative

(3) LifeBuilders Rallies

(4) Pastor's Prayer Partners

(5) Men of Legacy Program

(6) LifeBuilders Leadership Development Program

24. What is required for men to receive the LifeBuilders Discipleship100 Certificate and be recognized as a commissioned man?

Complete the following courses in small groups or personally:

- *LifeBuilders Essentials*
- *James: A Path to Discipleship*
- *Philippians: A Path to Joy*
- *Maximized Manhood*
- *Courage*
- *How to Develop a Powerful Prayer Life*
- *Characters with Character*

25. What is required for men to receive the LifeBuilders Discipleship 200 Certificate?

- *Never Quit*
- *Sexual Integrity*
- *Daring*
- *The Power of Potential*
- *Treasure*
- *Real Man*
- *Strong Men in Tough Times*

26. Name six opportunities for ministry training and involvement

- *Chaplains Community*
- *Operation Compassion*
- *Lay Leadership Development*
- *Men of Action*

- *Certificate in Ministerial Studies (CIMS*
- *Men On a Mission*

27. What is step one to connecting with new men?

Meet with pastor and plan a strategy

28. Name five natural ministry times to build relationships with men and get them into LifeBuilders Discipleship Ministry.

- Altar
- Baby Dedications provide opportunities for LifeBuilders men to connect with new fathers.
- Every worship service
- Top Ten Card
- Weddings
- Times of bereavement, sickness, or need
- Work days
- Softball, fishing tournaments, golf tournaments, other activities that draw men
- Community outreach events
- Have cards made with a personal invitation to a special event. Give each man one card to give to another man to participate in the event.
- Resurrection Breakfast
- Mission Teams
- Prayer Ministries
- Men's Retreats
- LifeBuilders Rally
- Greeters & Ushers Ministry

29. How many momentum-building events should be planned annually?

Plan two major momentum-building events each year to draw new men.

Plan four other momentum-building events to keep momentum to draw new men.